NARRATIVE OF THE LIFE OF FREDERICK DOUGLASS

Frederick Douglass

EDITORIAL DIRECTOR Justin Kestler
EXECUTIVE EDITOR Ben Florman

SERIES EDITORS Boomie Aglietti, John Crowther, Justin Kestler
PRODUCTION Christian Lorentzen

WRITER Laura Heffernan
EDITORS Matt Blanchard, John Crowther

This edition published by Spark Publishing

Spark Publishing
A Division of SparkNotes LLC
120 Fifth Avenue, 8th Floor
New York, NY 10011

02 03 04 05 SN 9 8 7 6 5 4 3 2 1

Please send all comments and questions or report errors to feedback@sparknotes.com.

Library of Congress information available upon request

Printed and bound in the United States

RRD-C

ISBN 1-58663-815-7

INTRODUCTION: STOPPING TO BUY SPARKNOTES ON A SNOWY EVENING

Whose words these are you *think* you know.
Your paper's due tomorrow, though;
We're glad to see you stopping here
To get some help before you go.

Lost your course? You'll find it here.
Face tests and essays without fear.
Between the words, good grades at stake:
Get great results throughout the year.

Once school bells caused your heart to quake
As teachers circled each mistake.
Use SparkNotes and no longer weep,
Ace every single test you take.

Yes, books are lovely, dark, and deep,
But only what you grasp you keep,
With hours to go before you sleep,
With hours to go before you sleep.

Contents

CONTEXT

FREDERICK DOUGLASS WAS BORN into slavery in Maryland as Frederick Bailey circa 1818. Douglass served as a slave on farms on the Eastern Shore of Maryland and in Baltimore throughout his youth. In Baltimore, especially, Douglas enjoyed relatively more freedom than slaves usually did in the South. In the city, Douglass first learned how to read and began making contacts with educated free blacks.

Douglass eventually escaped north to New York at the age of about twenty. Here he reunited with and married his fiancée, a free black woman from Baltimore named Anna Murray. Uneasy about Douglass's fugitive status, the two finally settled further north in New Bedford, Massachusetts, and Frederick changed his last name from Bailey to Douglass. Douglass worked for the next three years as a laborer and continued his self-education.

In the early 1840s, the abolitionist, or anti-slavery, movement was gaining momentum, especially in the far Northeast. When Douglass first arrived in Massachusetts, he began reading the *Liberator,* the abolitionist newspaper edited by William Lloyd Garrison. In 1841, Douglass attended an abolitionist meeting in Nantucket, Massachusetts, where he met Garrison and was encouraged to tell the crowd about his experiences of slavery. Douglass's spoken account was so well-received that Garrison offered to employ him as an abolitionist speaker for the American Anti-Slavery Society.

From 1841 to 1845, Douglass traveled extensively with Garrison and others through the Northern states, speaking nearly every day on the injustice and brutality of slavery. Douglass encountered hostile opposition and, most often, the charge that he was lying. Many Americans did not believe that such an eloquent and intelligent Negro had so recently been a slave.

Douglass encountered a different brand of opposition within the ranks of the Anti-Slavery Society itself. He was one of only a few black men employed by the mostly white society, and the society's leaders, including Garrison, would often condescendingly insist that Douglass merely relate the "facts" of his experience, and leave the philosophy, rhetoric, and persuasive argument to others. Douglass's 1845 *Narrative of the Life of Frederick Douglass, An American Slave, Written by Himself* can be seen as a response to both of these types of opposition. The *Narrative* pointedly states that Douglass is its sole author, and it contains two prefaces from Garrison and another abolitionist, Wendell Phillips, to attest to this fact. Douglass's use of the true names of people and places further silenced his detractors who questioned the truthfulness of his story and status as a former slave. Additionally, the *Narrative* undertook to be not only a personal account of Douglass's experiences as a slave, but also an eloquent antislavery treatise. With the *Narrative*, Douglass demonstrated his ability to be not only the teller of his story, but its interpreter as well.

Because Douglass did use real names in his *Narrative*, he had to flee the United States for a time, as his Maryland "owner" was legally entitled to track him down in Massachusetts and reclaim him. Douglass spent the next two years traveling in the British Isles, where he was warmly received. He returned to the United States only after two English friends purchased his freedom. His reputation at home had grown during his absence. The *Narrative* was an instant bestseller in 1845 and went through five print runs to accommodate demand. Despite opposition from Garrison, Douglass started his own abolitionist newspaper in 1847 in Rochester, New York, under the name *North Star.*

Douglass continued to write and lecture against slavery and also devoted attention to the women's rights movement. He became involved in politics, to the disapproval of other abolitionists who avoided politics for ideological reasons. When the Civil War broke out in 1861, Douglass campaigned first to make it the aim of the war to abolish slavery and then to allow black men to fight for the Union. He was successful on both fronts: Lincoln issued the Emancipation Proclamation on December 31, 1862, and Congress authorized the enlistment of black men in 1863, though they were paid only half what white soldiers made. The Union won the Civil War on April 9, 1865.

During the 1860s and beyond, Douglass continued to campaign, now for the right of blacks to vote and receive equal treatment in public places. Douglass served in government positions under several administrations in the 1870s and 1880s. He also found time to publish the third volume of his autobiography, *The Life and Times of Frederick Douglass*, in 1881 (the second volume, *My Bondage and My Freedom*, was published in 1855). In 1882, Douglass's wife, Anna, died. He remarried, to Helen Pitts, a white advocate of the women's movement, in 1884. Douglass died of a heart attack in 1895.

Until the 1960s, Douglass's *Narrative* was largely ignored by critics and historians, who focused instead on the speeches for which Douglass was primarily known. Yet Douglass's talent clearly extended to the written word. His *Narrative* emerged in a popular tradition of slave narratives and slavery fictions that includes Harriet Beecher Stowe's *Uncle Tom's Cabin* and Harriet Jacobs's *Incidents in the Life of a Slave Girl*. Douglass's work is read today as one of the finest examples of the slave-narrative genre. Douglass co-opted narrative styles and forms from the spiritual conversion narrative, the sentimental novel, oratorical rhetoric, and heroic fiction. He took advantage of the popularity of slave narratives while expanding the possibilities of those narratives. Finally, in its somewhat unique depiction of slavery as an assault on selfhood and in its attention to the tensions of becoming an individual, Douglass's *Narrative* can be read as a contribution to the literary tradition of American Romantic individualism.

Plot Overview

FREDERICK DOUGLASS WAS BORN into slavery sometime in
1817 or 1818. Like many slaves, he is unsure of his exact
date of birth. Douglass is separated from his mother, Harriet Bailey, soon after he is born. His father is most likely
their white master, Captain Anthony. Captain Anthony is
the clerk of a rich man named Colonel Lloyd. Lloyd owns hundreds
of slaves, who call his large, central plantation the "Great House
Farm." Life on any of Lloyd's plantations, like that on many Southern plantations, is brutal. Slaves are overworked and exhausted,
receive little food, few articles of clothing, and no beds. Those who
break rules—and even those who do not—are beaten or whipped,
and sometimes even shot by the plantation overseers, the cruelest of
which are Mr. Severe and Mr. Austin Gore.

Douglass's life on this plantation is not as hard as that of most of
the other slaves. Being a child, he serves in the household instead of
in the fields. At the age of seven, he is given to Captain Anthony's
son-in-law's brother, Hugh Auld, who lives in Baltimore. In Baltimore, Douglass enjoys a relatively freer life. In general, city slave-
owners are more conscious of appearing cruel or neglectful toward
their slaves in front of their non-slaveowning neighbors.

Sophia Auld, Hugh's wife, has never had slaves before, and therefore she is surprisingly kind to Douglass at first. She even begins to
teach Douglass to read, until her husband orders her to stop, saying
that education makes slaves unmanageable. Eventually, Sophia suc-
cumbs to the mentality of slaveowning and loses her natural kindli-
ness. Though Sophia and Hugh Auld become crueler toward him,
Douglass still likes Baltimore and is able to teach himself to read with
the help of local boys. As he learns to read and write, Douglass
becomes conscious of the evils of slavery and of the existence of the
abolitionist, or antislavery, movement. He resolves to escape to the
North eventually.

After the deaths of Captain Anthony and his remaining heirs,
Douglass is taken back to serve Thomas Auld, Captain Anthony's
son-in-law. Auld is a mean man made harsher by his false religious
piety. Auld considers Douglass unmanageable, so Auld rents him
for one year to Edward Covey, a man known for "breaking" slaves.
Covey manages, in the first six months, to work and whip all the

5

spirit out of Douglass. Douglass becomes a brutish man, no longer interested in reading or freedom, capable only of resting from his injuries and exhaustion. The turning point comes when Douglass resolves to fight back against Covey. The two men have a two-hour fight, after which Covey never touches Douglass again.

His year with Covey over, Douglass is next rented to William Freeland for two years. Though Freeland is a milder, fairer man, Douglass's will to escape is nonetheless renewed. At Freeland's, Douglass begins educating his fellow slaves in a Sabbath school at the homes of free blacks. Despite the threat of punishment and violence they face, many slaves from neighboring farms come to Douglass and work diligently to learn. At Freeland's, Douglass also forms a plan of escape with three fellow slaves with whom he is close. Someone betrays their plan to Freeland, however, and Douglass and the others are taken to jail. Thomas Auld then sends Douglass back to Baltimore with Hugh Auld, to learn the trade of ship caulking.

In Baltimore's trade industry, Douglass runs up against strained race relations. White workers have been working alongside free black workers, but the whites have begun to fear that the increasing numbers of free blacks will take their jobs. Though only an apprentice and still a slave, Douglass encounters violent tactics of intimidation from his white coworkers and is forced to switch shipyards. In his new apprenticeship, Douglass quickly learns the trade of caulking and soon earns the highest wages possible, always turning them over to Hugh Auld.

Eventually, Douglass receives permission from Hugh Auld to hire out his extra time. He saves money bit by bit and eventually makes his escape to New York. Douglass refrains from describing the details of his escape in order to protect the safety of future slaves who may attempt the journey. In New York, Douglass fears recapture and changes his name from Bailey to Douglass. Soon after, he marries Anna Murray, a free woman he met while in Baltimore. They move north to Massachusetts, where Douglass becomes deeply engaged with the abolitionist movement as both a writer and an orator.

CHARACTER LIST

Frederick Douglass The author and narrator of the *Narrative*. Douglass, a rhetorically skilled and spirited man, is a powerful orator for the abolitionist movement. One of his reasons for writing the *Narrative* is to offer proof to critics who felt that such an articulate and intelligent man could not have once been a slave. The *Narrative* describes Douglass's experience under slavery from his early childhood until his escape North at the age of twenty. Within that time, Douglass progresses from unenlightened victim of the dehumanizing practices of slavery to educated and empowered young man. He gains the resources and convictions to escape to the North and wage a political fight against the institution of slavery.

Captain Anthony Douglass's first master and probably his father. Anthony is the clerk for Colonel Lloyd, managing Lloyd's surrounding plantations and the overseers of those plantations. Anthony is a cruel man who takes pleasure in whipping his slaves, especially Douglass's Aunt Hester. He is called "Captain" because he once piloted ships up the Chesapeake Bay.

Colonel Edward Lloyd Captain Anthony's boss and Douglass's first owner. Colonel Lloyd is an extremely rich man who owns all of the slaves and lands where Douglass grows up. Lloyd insists on extreme subservience from his slaves and often punishes them unjustly.

Lucretia Auld Captain Anthony's daughter and Thomas Auld's wife. After Captain Anthony's death, Lucretia inherits half his property, including Douglass. Lucretia is as cruel an owner as her husband.

Captain Thomas Auld Lucretia Auld's husband and Hugh Auld's brother. Thomas Auld did not grow up owning slaves, but gained them through his marriage to Lucretia. After attending a church meeting in Maryland, Thomas Auld becomes a "pious" man, but he uses his newfound Christianity to be even more self-righteously brutal toward his slaves.

Hugh Auld Thomas Auld's brother and Douglass's occasional master. Hugh lives in Baltimore with his wife, Sophia. Thomas and Lucretia Auld allow Hugh to borrow Douglass as a servant for Hugh's son, Thomas. Hugh is well aware that whites maintain power over blacks by depriving them of education, and he unwittingly enlightens Douglass in this matter. Hugh is not as cruel as his brother Thomas, but he becomes harsher due to a drinking habit in his later years. Hugh seems to suffer some consciousness that slavery and the law's treatment of blacks are inhumane, but he does not allow this consciousness to interfere with his exercising power over Douglass.

Sophia Auld Hugh Auld's wife. Sophia was a working woman before marrying Hugh, and she had never owned slaves. The corruption of owning a slave transforms Sophia from a sympathetic, kind woman into a vengeful monster.

Edward Covey A notorious slave "breaker" and Douglass's keeper for one year. Slave owners send their unruly slaves to Covey, who works and punishes them (thus getting free labor to cultivate his rented land) and returns them trained and docile. Covey's tactics as a slaveholder are both cruel and sneaky. He is deliberately deceptive and devious when interacting with his slaves, creating an atmosphere of constant surveillance and fear.

Betsy Bailey Douglass's grandmother. Betsy raised Douglass on Captain Anthony's land after Douglass's mother was taken away. Betsy served the Anthony family her whole life and had many children and grandchildren who became slaves for the Anthonys. After seeing Captain Anthony's children from birth to death, Betsy is abandoned to a hut in the woods instead of being allowed to go free.

Aunt Hester Douglass's aunt. Aunt Hester is an exceptionally beautiful and noble-looking woman, superior to most white and black women. Captain Anthony is extraordinarily interested in Hester, and she therefore suffers countless whippings at his hands.

Harriet Bailey Douglass's mother. Harriet is separated from Douglass after his birth, but she still attempts to maintain family relations by walking twelve miles to see him at night. She dies when Douglass is young.

Sandy Jenkins A slave acquaintance of Douglass. The highly superstitious Sandy stands in the *Narrative* as a representative of all uneducated, superstitious slaves. Sandy is kind to Douglass when Douglass runs away from Covey's, but the *Narrative* also implies that Sandy may have informed William Freeland about Douglass's plans to escape.

William Freeland Douglass's keeper for two years following his time with Covey. Freeland is the most fair and straightforward of all Douglass's masters and is not hypocritically pious. Douglass acknowledges Freeland's exceptional fairness with a pun on his name—"free land."

William Hamilton Father-in-law of Thomas Auld. After Lucretia Auld's death, Thomas remarries Hamilton's oldest daughter. Hamilton himself sometimes takes charge of Douglass, as when Hamilton arrests Douglass for plotting to escape from Freeland.

William Gardner A Baltimore shipbuilder. Hugh Auld sends Douglass to Gardner to learn the trade of caulking. Gardner's shipyard is disorderly with racial tension between free-black carpenters and white carpenters, and Gardner is under pressure to complete several ships for a deadline.

Anna Murray Douglass's wife. Anna is a free black woman from Baltimore who becomes engaged to Douglass before he escapes to freedom. After his escape, Anna and Douglass marry in New York and then move to New Bedford, Massachusetts.

Nathan Johnson A Massachusetts worker and abolitionist. Johnson is immediately kind and helpful to the Douglasses, loaning them money, helping Douglass find work, and suggesting Douglass's new name. Johnson is well informed on national politics and keeps a nice household.

William Lloyd Garrison Founder of the American Anti-Slavery Society. Garrison meets Douglass when Douglass is persuaded to tell his history at an abolitionist convention in Nantucket in 1841. Immediately impressed with Douglass's poise and with the power of his story, Garrison hires him for the abolitionist cause.

Wendell Phillips President of the American Anti-Slavery Society. Phillips considers Douglass a close friend. He admires Douglass's bravery in publishing his history without pseudonyms, but also fears for Douglass's safety.

ANALYSIS OF MAJOR CHARACTERS

FREDERICK DOUGLASS

In the *Narrative,* Douglass acts as both the narrator and the protagonist, and he appears quite different in these two roles. The wide gulf between Douglass's two personas is, in fact, the point of the *Narrative*: Douglass progresses from uneducated, oppressed slave to worldly and articulate political commentator. Douglass frequently dramatizes the difference between his older, more experienced self and his younger self through references to his relative ignorance and naïveté. One instance of this dramatization occurs when Douglass mocks how impressed he was as a young man to encounter the city of Annapolis—a city that now seems small to him by the standards of Northern industrial cities.

As the narrator, Douglass presents himself as a reasoned, rational figure. His tone is dry and he does not exaggerate. He is capable of seeing both sides of an issue, even the issue of slavery. Though he makes no excuses for slave owners, he does make an effort to present a realistic—if critical—account of how and why slavery operates. His humane vision allows him to separate slaveowning individuals from the institution that corrupts them. Moreover, Douglass as the narrator presents himself as capable of intricate and deep feeling. He allows his narrative to linger over the inexpressible emotions he and others have suffered, and he sometimes dramatizes his own tears.

Douglass as the protagonist of the *Narrative* is sometimes a strong character and at other times a sidelined presence. Douglass's strength as a character fluctuates because Douglass the narrator sometimes presents his younger self as an interesting, unique case and sometimes as a typical, representative American slave. As a representative slave, Douglass's individual characteristics matter less than the similarity of his circumstances to those of all other slaves, as when he describes the circumstances of his upbringing in Chapter I of the *Narrative*. Similarly, at times Douglass exists merely as a witness to scenes featuring other characters. These scenes are important to the *Narrative* not because of Douglass's role in them, but because they present a composite portrait of the dehumanizing aspects of slavery.

Generally, Douglass the protagonist becomes a stronger presence as the *Narrative* proceeds. The protagonist Douglass exists in the *Narrative* as a character in process and flux, formed and reformed by such pivotal scenes as Captain Anthony's whipping of Aunt Hester, Hugh Auld's insistence that Douglass not be taught to read, and Douglass's fight with Covey. Aunt Hester's whipping introduces Douglass to the physical and psychic cruelty of slavery. He becomes committed to literacy after Hugh Auld's order that Sophia Auld cease teaching him. Douglass then is reintegrated into slavery and loses his desire to learn at Thomas Auld's and at Covey's. Finally, Douglass reestablishes a sense of self and justice through his fight with Covey. Douglass thus emerges as a figure formed negatively by slavery and cruelty, and positively by literacy education and a controlled but aggressive insistence on rights.

Through this process, certain traits remain constant in young Douglass's character. Though often isolated and alienated, Douglass remains largely optimistic about his fate and maintains a strong spiritual sense. He is exceptionally resourceful, as demonstrated by his untraditional self-education. Finally, Douglass has a strong desire to help others, expressed in part through his commitment to improving the lives of his fellow slaves, as we see in the Sabbath school he runs while under the ownership of William Freeland.

SOPHIA AULD

Sophia Auld is one of the few characters, apart from Douglass himself, who changes throughout the course of the *Narrative*. Specifically, Sophia is transformed from a kind, caring woman who owns no slaves to an excessively cruel slave owner. On the one hand, she appears more realistic and humane than other characters because we see her character in process. On the other hand, Sophia comes to resemble less a character than an illustration of Douglass's argument about slavery. Douglass uses the instance of Sophia's transformation from kind to cruel as a message about the negative effects of slavery on slaveholders. Sophia also seems less realistic as a character because Douglass's descriptions of her are rhetorically dramatic rather than realistic. Douglass's initial description of Sophia idealizes her kind features, and his description of her character post-transformation equally dramatizes her demonic qualities.

Sophia's gender affects her characterization in the *Narrative*. To nineteenth-century readers, it would have seemed natural for Sophia, as a female, to be sympathetic and loving. Consequently, it would have appeared all the more unnatural and undesirable for her to be transformed into an evil slave owner. Because many nineteenth-century readers thought of maternal figures as the symbol of their society's moral righteousness, corruption of a maternal figure—or disruption of her family structure—would point directly to moral problems in the society at large. In this regard, Sophia appears in the *Narrative* as a symbolic character as well as a realistic character. Her symbolism of a culture's corruption is an important emotional component of Douglass's larger argument against slavery.

EDWARD COVEY

Edward Covey represents Douglass's nemesis in the *Narrative*. Covey is a typical villain figure in that his cruelty is calculated. He is not a victim of the slavery mentality but a naturally evil man who finds an outlet for his cruelty in slaveholding. Covey is skilled and methodical in his physical punishment of his slaves, but he is even more skilled at psychological cruelty. While other slaveholders in the *Narrative* can be deceitful with their slaves, Covey uses deception as his primary method of dealing with them. He makes the slaves feel that they are under constant surveillance by lying to them and creeping around the fields in an effort to catch them being lazy.

One way in which Douglass portrays Covey as a villain is by depicting him as anti-Christian. The slaves call Covey "the snake," in part because he sneaks through the grass, but also because this nickname is a reference to Satan's appearance in the form of a snake in the biblical book of Genesis. Douglass also presents Covey as a false Christian. Covey tries to deceive himself and God into believing that he is a true Christian, but his evil actions reveal him to be a sinner. As Douglass associates himself with Christian faith, he heightens the sense of conflict between himself and Covey by showing Covey to be an enemy of Christianity itself.

As Douglass's nemesis, Covey is the chief figure against whom Douglass defines himself. Douglass's fight with Covey is the climax of the *Narrative*—it marks Douglass's turning point from demoralized slave to confident, freedom-seeking man. Douglass achieves this transformation by matching and containing Covey's own violence and by showing himself to be Covey's opposite. Douglass thus emerges as brave man, while Covey is exposed as a coward. Douglass is shown to be capable of restraint, while Covey is revealed to be an excessive braggart. Finally, Douglass emerges as a leader of men, while Covey is shown to be an ineffectual master who cannot even enlist the aid of another slave, Bill, to help him.

Themes, Motifs & Symbols

Themes

Themes are the fundamental and often universal ideas explored in a literary work.

Ignorance as a Tool of Slavery

Douglass's *Narrative* shows how white slaveholders perpetuate slavery by keeping their slaves ignorant. At the time Douglass was writing, many people believed that slavery was a natural state of being. They believed that blacks were inherently incapable of participating in civil society and thus should be kept as workers for whites. The *Narrative* explains the strategies and procedures by which whites gain and keep power over blacks from their birth onward. Slave owners keep slaves ignorant of basic facts about themselves, such as their birth date or their paternity. This enforced ignorance robs children of their natural sense of individual identity. As slave children grow older, slave owners prevent them from learning how to read and write, as literacy would give them a sense of self-sufficiency and capability. Slaveholders understand that literacy would lead slaves to question the right of whites to keep slaves. Finally, by keeping slaves illiterate, Southern slaveholders maintain control over what the rest of America knows about slavery. If slaves cannot write, their side of the slavery story cannot be told. Wendell Phillips makes this point in his prefatory letter to the *Narrative*.

Knowledge as the Path to Freedom

Just as slave owners keep men and women as slaves by depriving them of knowledge and education, slaves must seek knowledge and education in order to pursue freedom. It is from Hugh Auld that Douglass learns this notion that knowledge must be the way to freedom, as Auld forbids his wife to teach Douglass how to read and write because education ruins slaves. Douglass sees that Auld has unwittingly revealed the strategy by which whites manage to keep blacks as slaves and by which blacks might free themselves. Douglass presents his own self-education as the primary means by which he is able to free himself, and as his greatest tool to work for the freedom of all slaves.

Though Douglass himself gains his freedom in part by virtue of his self-education, he does not oversimplify this connection. Douglass has no illusions that knowledge automatically renders slaves free. Knowledge helps slaves to articulate the injustice of slavery to themselves and others, and helps them to recognize themselves as men rather than slaves. Rather than provide immediate freedom, this awakened consciousness brings suffering, as Hugh Auld predicts. Once slaves are able to articulate the injustice of slavery, they come to loathe their masters, but still cannot physically escape without meeting great danger.

SLAVERY'S DAMAGING EFFECT ON SLAVEHOLDERS

In the *Narrative*, Douglass shows slaveholding to be damaging not only to the slaves themselves, but to slave owners as well. The corrupt and irresponsible power that slave owners enjoy over their slaves has a detrimental effect on the slave owners' own moral health. With this theme, Douglass completes his overarching depiction of slavery as unnatural for all involved.

Douglass describes typical behavior patterns of slaveholders to depict the damaging effects of slavery. He recounts how many slave-owning men have been tempted to adultery and rape, fathering children with their female slaves. Such adultery threatens the unity of the slave owner's family, as the father is forced to either sell or perpetually punish his own child, while the slave owner's wife becomes resentful and cruel. In other instances, slave owners such as Thomas Auld develop a perverted religious sense to remain blind to the sins they commit in their own home. Douglass's main illustration of the corruption of slave owners is Sophia Auld. The irresponsible power of slaveholding transforms Sophia from an idealistic woman to a demon. By showing the detrimental effects of slaveholding on Thomas Auld, Sophia Auld, and others, Douglass implies that slavery should be outlawed for the greater good of all society.

SLAVEHOLDING AS A PERVERSION OF CHRISTIANITY

Over the course of the *Narrative*, Douglass develops a distinction between true Christianity and false Christianity. Douglass clarifies the point in his appendix, calling the former "the Christianity of Christ" and the latter "the Christianity of this land." Douglass shows that slaveholders' Christianity is not evidence of their innate goodness, but merely a hypocritical show that serves to bolster their self-righteous brutality. To strike this distinction, Douglass points to the basic contradiction between the charitable, peaceful tenets of Christianity and the violent, immoral actions of slaveholders.

The character of Thomas Auld stands as an illustration of this theme. Like Sophia Auld, Thomas undergoes a transformation in the *Narrative* from cruel slave owner to even crueler slave owner. Douglass demonstrates that Auld's brutality increases after he becomes a "pious" man, as Auld's show of piety increases his confidence in his "God-given" right to hold and mistreat slaves. Through the instance of Auld, Douglass also demonstrates that the Southern church itself is corrupt. Auld's church benefits from Auld's money, earned by means of slaves. Thus Auld's church, like many Southern churches, is complicit in the inhuman cruelty of slavery.

MOTIFS

Motifs are recurring structures, contrasts, or literary devices that can help to develop and inform the text's major themes.

THE VICTIMIZATION OF FEMALE SLAVES
Women often appear in Douglass's *Narrative* not as full characters, but as vivid images—specifically, images of abused bodies. Douglass's Aunt Hester, Henrietta and Mary, and Henny, for example, appear only in scenes that demonstrate their masters' abuse of them. Douglass's depcitions of the women's mangled and emaciated bodies are meant to incite pain and outrage in the reader and point to the unnaturalness of the institution of slavery.

THE TREATMENT OF SLAVES AS PROPERTY
Throughout the *Narrative,* Douglass is concerned with showing the discrepancy between the fact that slaves are human beings and the fact that slave owners treat them as property. Douglass shows how slaves frequently are passed between owners, regardless of where the slaves' families are. Slave owners value slaves only to the extent that they can perform productive labor; they often treat slaves like livestock, mere animals, without reason. Douglass presents this treatment of humans as objects or animals as cruel and absurd.

FREEDOM IN THE CITY

Douglass's *Narrative* switches settings several times between the rural Eastern Shore of Maryland and the city of Baltimore. Baltimore is a site of relative freedom for Douglass and other slaves. This freedom results from the standards of decency set by the non-slave-holding segment of the urban population—standards that generally prevent slaveholders from demonstrating extreme cruelty toward their slaves. The city also stands as a place of increased possibility and a more open society. It is in Baltimore that Douglass meets for the first time whites who oppose slavery and who regard Douglass as a human being. By contrast, the countryside is a place of heightened surveillance of slaves by slaveholders. In the countryside, slaves enjoy the least amount of freedom and mobility.

SYMBOLS

Symbols are objects, characters, figures, or colors used to represent abstract ideas or concepts.

WHITE-SAILED SHIPS

Douglass encounters white-sailed ships moving up the Chesapeake Bay during the spiritual and physical low point of his first months with Covey. The ships appear almost as a vision to Douglass, and he recognizes them as a sign or message about his demoralized state. The ships, traveling northward from port to port, seem to represent freedom from slavery to Douglass. Their white sails, which Douglass associates with angels, also suggest spiritualism—or the freedom that comes with spiritualism.

SANDY'S ROOT

Sandy Jenkins offers Douglass a root from the forest with supposedly magical qualities that help protect slaves from whippings. Douglass does not seem to believe in the magical powers of the root, but he uses it to appease Sandy. In fact, Douglass states in a footnote that Sandy's belief in the root is "superstitious" and typical of the more ignorant slave population. In this regard, the root stands as a symbol of a traditional African approach to religion and belief.

The Columbian Orator

Douglass first encounters *The Columbian Orator*, a collection of political essays, poems, and dialogues, around the age of twelve, just after he has learned to read. As Douglass becomes educated in the rudimentary skills of literacy, he also becomes educated about the injustice of slavery. Of all the pieces in *The Columbian Orator*, Douglass focuses on the master-slave dialogue and the speech on behalf of Catholic emancipation. These pieces help Douglass to articulate why slavery is wrong, both philosophically and politically. *The Columbian Orator*, then, becomes a symbol not only of human rights, but also of the power of eloquence and articulation. To some extent, Douglass sees his own life's work as an attempt to replicate *The Columbian Orator*.

SYMBOLS

SUMMARY & ANALYSIS

PREFACE BY WILLIAM LLOYD GARRISON & LETTER FROM WENDELL PHILLIPS

SUMMARY: PREFACE BY WILLIAM LLOYD GARRISON
William Lloyd Garrison, founder of the American Anti-Slavery Society, describes his first encounter with Frederick Douglass at an anti-slavery convention in Nantucket, Massachusetts, in 1841. This encounter led to a long partnership between Douglass and the Anti-Slavery Society. At the convention, Douglass spoke to the audience about his life under slavery, and the audience responded powerfully to Douglass's impressive physical presence and intellectual demeanor. Garrison recalls rising after Douglass's speech and declaring it a better piece of oration, even, than the speech of the Patrick Henry during the time of the American Revolution. Garrison describes the audience's resounding positive response after Garrison asked them for a commitment to protect Douglass from slave owners.

Garrison recalls immediately recruiting Douglass as an anti-slavery promoter to aid the abolitionist cause and to make American audiences question their prejudice against blacks. Since Garrison recruited him, Douglass has been a successful and persuasive speaker. Douglass's prestige is due to his perfect union of head and heart, which helps him capture the hearts and convince the minds of others. Douglass's career proves wrong those who insist that the Negro race is naturally inferior. Garrison argues that any race would have become as degraded as the Negro race, had they been subjected to slavery. He relates the case of a shipwrecked white man who was kept in slavery in Africa for three years. When the man was found, he was unable to remember his native language and his powers of reason. Thus mental deterioration is a result of slavery, not a preexisting quality of the slave population.

Garrison attests that the *Narrative* is entirely Douglass's own work and is entirely truthful. Garrison compliments the *Narrative*'s literary merit, specifically its power to emotionally affect readers. He points specifically to the passage of Douglass's soliloquy on the banks of the Chesapeake Bay as evidence of Douglass's sublime mind. Garrison points out that as bad as Douglass's experiences have been, many slaves suffer even more. Garrison asks rhetorically how the practice of slavery, revealed to be evil, can be allowed to continue. He deplores the skeptics who refuse to believe in the brutality of the institution of slavery even when faced with evidence of its deprivation, physical cruelty, and sexual abuse. He anticipates that such skeptics will attempt to discredit Douglass, but will inevitably fail in the face of the candid truthfulness of the *Narrative*.

Garrison discusses the troubling issue of white men killing slaves and suffering no consequences. Douglass cites two cases of this in his *Narrative,* and Garrison points to another recent case in Maryland. Garrison reminds readers that this kind of murder happens frequently and goes unpunished, as black men and women are not allowed to testify against whites. Finally, he addresses and supports Douglass's particular rejection of the false Christianity of slaveholders. Garrison exhorts readers to repudiate slaveholders and join in support of the victims of slavery, as this is the side of God and faith.

SUMMARY: LETTER FROM WENDELL PHILLIPS
Wendell Phillips, abolitionist and president of the American Anti-Slavery Society, writes to Douglass as a friend. Phillips is relieved that factual accounts of the experiences of slaves are now being published so that the history of slavery can be fully revealed. Previously the histories of slavery consisted only of the selective information released by slaveholders. Phillips values Douglass's *Narrative* as an example of a slave awakening to his rights and as a description of slavery's particular campaign against the souls of slaves. Phillips considers it remarkable that Douglass's account originates in an area of the United States where slavery is said to be less harsh, thus attesting to unthinkable cruelty that must be experienced by those slaves in the Deep South.

Phillips attests that Douglass's *Narrative* is neither exaggerated nor unjust. The particular instances of cruelty that Douglass experienced and witnessed are not anomalies, but fundamental parts of the institution of slavery. Phillips fears for Douglass, who has written the true names of himself and his masters and has thus put himself in danger of recapture. Phillips draws a parallel between Douglass and the fathers of the Declaration of Independence who jeopardized their lives by signing their names. Phillips knows that

Douglass will be shielded by those abolitionists in the North who deliberately scorn the Fugitive Slave Laws, but this gesture is not enough. Massachusetts must soon explicitly declare itself an asylum for fugitive slaves.

Analysis: Preface by William Lloyd Garrison & Letter from Wendell Phillips

Slave narratives often begin with prefaces, written by white editors, that attempt to prepare white audiences for the narrative itself. Such prefaces usually testify to the authenticity of the narrative—the truth of its facts and the credibility of its black authorship. Because the editors position themselves as authorities on the narratives, the prefaces implicitly place black narratives under the control of white editors. Garrison's preface in particular displays the urge to control and contain Douglass's career and narrative. Garrison places himself at the center of the text. Douglass's success story is replaced somewhat by the story of Garrison's judgment and fostering of Douglass's talent. Thus when Garrison recalls Douglass's first speech at the Nantucket antislavery meeting, he does not reproduce any of Douglass's words. Instead, he expounds on his own small speech after Douglass's. Garrison's speech champions Douglass's abilities, but it also assumes the right to pass judgment on the quality of Douglass's speech. Garrison controls and contains Douglass's speech by placing it in comparison to historical references familiar to white audiences—the context of the American revolutionaries.

Garrison's and Phillips's prefaces also present Douglass's *Narrative* as a contribution to the political and philosophical argument against slavery. Both prefaces contain political arguments in favor of abolition and refutations of pro-slavery arguments. For instance, both men specifically address critics who insist that the violence of slavery is exaggerated and that stories like Douglass's are uncommon. Phillips and Garrison each point out that Douglass had a relatively mild experience of slavery in Maryland, one of the less isolated and harsh slave states. Similarly, Garrison addresses those who argue that it is natural that Negroes be kept as slaves because they are naturally inferior. To refute this, Garrison cites the case of the white man who experienced significant mental deterioration when kept as a slave in Africa for three years. Garrison also points to Douglass as a specimen of superior manhood, offering up Douglass's refinement of feeling, complexity of thought, oratorical genius, and even his commanding physical presence as evidence to contradict the claim that Negro race is inferior.

Garrison suggests that Douglass's *Narrative* is powerful because it offers such a drastic double picture—the articulate, familiar, enlightened Douglass presents and interprets his unenlightened, oppressed self under slavery. This duality of the protagonist is common to the genre of autobiography. In autobiography, a necessary disparity exists between the author as teller and the author's younger self. The disparity between these two selves in Douglass's case is particularly extreme because his story is not simply about a young man maturing but a young man escaping the oppression of slavery and becoming educated. Garrison presents the huge disparity between Douglass the author and Douglass the slave as evidence of the unnaturalness of slavery.

Garrison hints at another doubleness in Douglass's *Narrative*—the fact that the *Narrative* is a story about Douglass's specific and personal life and experiences, but is also meant to stand politically as the experience of most slaves. Though Garrison acknowledges Douglass's unique abilities, Garrison also recognizes the necessity of reading the *Narrative* as a representative depiction of any soul under slavery. In his preface, Garrison implies this substitution of Douglass for all slaves. Garrison's appeal to the Nantucket crowd to protect Douglass is, then, an implicit appeal to protect all fugitive slaves and to work against the institution of slavery in general.

Both Garrison's and Phillips's prefaces suggest that the literary merit of Douglass's *Narrative* lies in its ability to move readers, sometimes to tears. Nineteenth-century readers commonly admired deep feeling and pathos, and sentimentalism was a popular literary and rhetorical genre. Sentimental fiction and oration sought to motivate readers and listeners to political action through sympathy with those suffering under oppression. Readers and writers valued emotional displays of weeping as evidence of earnest and intricate emotional awareness. Many believed that this emotional awareness was a necessary component of intellectual reason. Though sections of Garrison's and Douglass's prose may seem trite or teary to us today, they would have originally been evidence of genuine and moral feeling at the time in which the *Narrative* was written.

Chapters I–II

Summary: Chapter I

> *I received the tidings of [my mother's] death with much the same emotions I should have probably felt at the death of a stranger.*
>
> (See QUOTATIONS, p. 53)

Douglass was born in Talbot County, Maryland, though he does not know the year, as most slaves are not allowed to know their ages. Douglass remembers being unhappy and confused that white children knew their ages, but he was not allowed even to ask his own. He estimates, based on an overheard comment from his master, that he was born in or around 1818.

Douglass's mother is Harriet Bailey, daughter of Isaac and Betsey Bailey. Douglass is separated from his mother soon after birth—a common practice among slave owners. Douglass assumes that this custom is intended to break the natural bond of affection between mother and child. He recalls that he only saw his mother on the rare occasions when she could walk twelve miles after dark to lie next to him at night. Harriet dies when Douglass is about seven. He is told about it afterward and is hardly affected by the news.

Douglass knows only that his father is a white man, though many people say that his master is his father. He explains that slaveholders often impregnate their female slaves. A law ensures that mixed-race children become slaves like their mothers. Thus slaveholders actually profit from this practice of rape, as it increases the number of slaves they own. Douglass explains that such mixed-race slaves have a worse lot than other slaves, as the slaveholder's wife, insulted by their existence, ensures that they either suffer constantly or are sold off. Douglass considers that the existence of such a large population of mixed-race slaves contradicts arguments that justify American slavery through the supposed inferiority of the African race.

Douglass's first master is Captain Anthony. The Captain's overseer, Mr. Plummer, is a drunk and a cruel man who carries a whip and cudgel with him and often uses them on slaves. The Captain himself is cruel as well. Douglass recalls the Captain frequently whipping Douglass's Aunt Hester. Douglass recalls feeling like both a witness to and a participant in the abuse the first time he ever saw it. He remembers this moment as his introduction into the hellish world of slavery. Douglass cannot, even now, describe what he felt while watching Aunt Hester's whipping.

Douglass recalls a particularly violent episode of the Captain whipping Aunt Hester. The Captain calls for Hester at night and finds that she has gone out with a slave named Ned, against the Captain's orders. Douglass implies that the Captain has a particular sexual interest in Hester, who is quite beautiful. The Captain brings Hester home, strips her to the waist, ties her, and whips her until her blood drips on the floor. Young Douglass is so terrified by the scene that he hides in a closet, hoping he will not be whipped next.

SUMMARY: CHAPTER II

Douglass's master, Captain Anthony, has two sons, Andrew and Richard, and a daughter, Lucretia, who is married to Captain Thomas Auld. They all live together in one house on a central plantation owned by Colonel Lloyd. Colonel Lloyd employs Captain Anthony as superintendent, meaning that Anthony supervises all of Lloyd's overseers. Lloyd's plantations raise tobacco, corn, and wheat. Captain Anthony and his son-in-law, Captain Auld, take the goods by ship to sell in Baltimore.

Lloyd owns about three to four hundred slaves in total. All slaves report to Lloyd's central plantation for their monthly allowances of pork or fish and corn meal. Slaves receive one set of linen clothing for the year. Adult slaves receive one blanket, but no bed. The floor is uncomfortable, but the slaves are so exhausted from work that they hardly notice. The overseer of Captain Anthony's farm is Mr. Severe—an appropriate name for such a cruel man. After Severe dies, Mr. Hopkins replaces him as overseer. Hopkins is less cruel and profane than Severe and is considered a fair overseer.

All of Colonel Lloyd's slaves refer to the central plantation, on which Douglass grew up, as the "Great House Farm" because it resembles a small village. Slaves from other plantations feel privileged to be sent to the Great House Farm on an errand. Douglass likens these slaves to state representatives proud to serve in the American Congress.

Slaves on their way to the Great House Farm usually sing wild, spontaneous songs that sound both joyful and sad. Douglass explains that he did not know the underlying meaning of these songs while he was a slave, but now understands that the songs are a bitter complaint about slavery. Douglass is now often moved to tears hearing them, and it was while listening to the songs that he first begins to understand the evil of slavery. Northerners who believe that the slaves are singing out of happiness, he says, are misinformed.

> *I did not, when a slave, understand the deep meaning of those rude and apparently incoherent songs. . . .*
> (See QUOTATIONS, p. 54)

ANALYSIS: CHAPTERS I–II

The first paragraph of Douglass's *Narrative* demonstrates the double purpose of the work as both a personal account and a public argument. Douglass introduces the reader to his own circumstances—his birthplace and the fact that he does not know his own age. He then generalizes from his own experience, explaining that almost no slaves know their true ages. Next, Douglass takes this detail of his experience and analyzes it. He points out that slave owners deliberately keep their slaves ignorant, and that this is a tactic whites use to gain power over slaves. This is the recurrent structure Douglass uses in his *Narrative*: he presents his personal experience as a typical slave experience, and then usually makes an analytical point about the experience and what it tells us about how slavery works and why it is wrong.

The main tactic of Douglass's antislavery argument in the *Narrative* is to analyze the institution of slavery and show how and why it works. This analysis demystifies slavery and reveals its brutality and wrongness. To many people who were not abolitionists, slavery appeared an entirely natural practice. To them, religious and economic arguments had demonstrated that blacks were inherently inferior to whites and belonged as an enslaved labor force. Douglass makes a clear case that slavery is sustained not through the natural superiority of whites, but through many concrete and contrived strategies of gaining and holding power over blacks. For example, Douglass shows how slave owners make slaves vulnerable by taking them from their mothers. Blacks are not subhuman to begin with, but are dehumanized only by such cruel practices of slavery.

Douglass also intends to use the *Narrative* to expose the even more evil underside of slavery. He writes to educate white audiences about what really goes on at slave plantations, including more cruel and depraved behaviors. For example, he devotes several paragraphs in Chapter I to a discussion about white slave owners impregnating their slaves. Douglass's narrative technique here is not

sensationalist. He does not seek to overly shock or titillate his readers. He does not, for example, dwell on the implied rapes of black
women, but rather upon the practical fate of their children. He seeks
instead to present a practice and explain how it degrades both slaves
and slave owners. Douglass often returns to this theme, depicting
slavery as dehumanizing to both slaveholders and slaves.

Douglass associates his witnessing of Captain Anthony whipping
Aunt Hester with his mental initiation into the horror of slavery.
Douglass describes the effect of this scene upon his young self and
uses this scene to help explain how slavery works. Part of the pain for
Douglass was not simply watching the whipping, but being unable to
stop it. He presents slavery as not only a type of physical control, but
also a type of mental control. Slaves become virtual participants in
brutality because they are made to fear for their own safety too much
to stop it. Douglass highlights these psychologically damaging
effects of slavery as much as physical effects such as lash wounds.

The scene of Captain Anthony stripping and whipping Aunt
Hester is the first of several scenes that feature the abuse of women.
Douglass often uses scenes of the abuse of female slaves to depict the
brutality of slave owners. Together, these images of whipped or
beaten female bodies constitute a motif in Douglass's *Narrative*.
The motif serves as an emotionally affecting, rather than logic-
based, argument about the evils of slavery. Additionally, Douglass's
use of women in his imagery serves to safely distance Douglass himself from the dehumanized and demeaned body of the slave.

Douglass likewise maintains distance between himself and slavery in his commentary on slave songs. He explains that he did not
fully understand the meaning of the songs when he himself was a
slave, but can now recognize and interpret them as laments. Douglass's voice in the Narrative is authoritative, and this authority
comes from his standing as someone who has escaped mental and
physical slavery and embraced education and articulation. Douglass's position as mediator between slaves and the Northern white
reading audience rests on his doubleness of self. He must be both the
demeaned self who experienced slavery and the liberated, educated
self who can interpret the institution of slavery. This doubleness or
fracturing of self is not without consequences, though. In his analysis of the slave songs, Douglass exhibits a sense of nostalgia for
when he was part of the "circle" of singing slaves.

CHAPTERS III–IV

SUMMARY: CHAPTER III

Douglass continues detailing Colonel Lloyd's home plantation where he grew up. Lloyd has a large cultivated garden that people from all over Maryland come to see. Some slaves can not resist eating fruit out of it. To prevent them, Lloyd puts tar on the fence surrounding the garden and whips any slave found with tar on him.

Colonel Lloyd also has an impressive stable with horses and carriages. The stable is run by two slaves, a father and son named old Barney and young Barney. The Colonel is picky about his horses and often whips both men for minute faults in the horses that even they themselves cannot even control. Despite the injustice of this system, the slaves can never complain. Colonel Lloyd insists that his slaves stand silent and afraid while he speaks and that they receive punishment without comment. Douglass recalls seeing old Barney kneel on the ground and receive more than thirty lashes. The whippings are often performed by one of the Colonel's three sons or by one of his three sons-in-law.

Colonel Lloyd's wealth is so great that he has never even seen some of the hundreds of slaves he owns. One day, the Colonel meets a slave traveling on the road. Lloyd, without identifying himself, asks the slave about his owner and how well he is treated. The slave responds that his owner is Colonel Lloyd, and that he is not treated well. Several weeks later, the slave is chained and sold to a Georgia slave trader for the offense to Lloyd. This is the punishment, Douglass concludes, that awaits slaves who tell the truth.

Douglass explains that many slaves, if asked, always report being contented with their life and their masters, for fear of punishment. This suppression of the truth is common to all people, slaves or free. Slaves sometimes truthfully speak well of their masters, too. It is also common for slaves to become competitive and prejudiced about their masters. Slaves sometimes argue over whose master is kinder, even if the masters are not kind at all.

SUMMARY: CHAPTER IV

The second overseer at Captain Anthony's, Mr. Hopkins, is fired after only a short time and replaced by Mr. Austin Gore. Mr. Gore is proud, ambitious, cunning, and cruel, and his domination over the slaves is total. He does not argue or hear protests and sometimes provokes slaves only for an excuse to punish them. Mr. Gore thrives on the Great House Farm. His ensures that all of the slaves bow down to him, while he, in turn, willingly bows down to the Colonel. Mr. Gore is a silent man, never joking as some overseers would. He performs barbaric deeds of punishment with a cool demeanor.

One day, Mr. Gore whips a slave named Demby, who then runs into a nearby creek to soothe the pain. Demby refuses to come out of the creek, and Mr. Gore gives Demby a three-count to return. When Demby makes no response after each call, Mr. Gore promptly shoots him. When questioned about his actions, Mr. Gore calmly explains that Demby was setting a bad example for the rest of the slaves. Mr. Gore is never investigated for this murder, and he still lives free. Douglass points out with irony that Mr. Gore is respected for his talent as an overseer.

Douglass offers several examples similar to Mr. Gore's killing of Demby. Mr. Thomas Lanman of Maryland has boasted of violently killing two slaves, yet has never been investigated for the crimes. Also in Maryland, the wife of another slave owner beat Douglass's wife's cousin to death with a stick. The community issued a warrant for the arrest of the wife, but the warrant has never been served. Colonel Lloyd's neighbor, Mr. Beal Bondly, shot and killed an elderly slave of Colonel Lloyd's who was fishing on Bondly's property. Colonel Lloyd did not complain about the killing.

ANALYSIS: CHAPTERS III–IV

Because the *Narrative* is both an autobiography and a treatise against slavery, Douglass often incorporates general information, including stories about, or heard from, people that he knew. Therefore, several of the opening chapters of the *Narrative* do not focus on Douglass at all. In Chapters III and IV, Douglass focuses on Colonel Lloyd's impressive plantation. Such detail serves not only to set the scene for Douglass's childhood, but also to verify the authenticity of the *Narrative*. We must remember that many nineteenth-century readers—especially readers unsympathetic to the plight of slaves—would have doubted the authenticity of Douglass's *Narrative*. The public was particularly skeptical of Douglass because he was more articulate than they thought a slave could be. Douglass extensively uses details of setting and character to reinforce the truthfulness of his *Narrative*, as Garrison and Phillips both point out in their prefaces.

As Douglass spends so much time describing scenes featuring other figures, such as Demby, the *Narrative* at times resembles a picaresque novel rather than an autobiography. Picaresque novels typically feature a series of episodes held together simply because they all happened to a single character. Douglass is still the character holding together his disparate scenes, as he either witnessed or heard about each of them. Douglass's technique in rendering the scenes also invites the comparison to a picaresque novel. His depictions include novelistic detail, as when old Barney removes his hat to reveal his bald head before being whipped. Similarly, Douglass's depiction of Mr. Gore shooting Demby has the dramatic sequence of fiction. Douglass shows us the scene, recounting each of Mr. Gore's three counts and Demby's reaction after each count.

Douglass also uses the stories of other slaves to make an argument about the inhumanity of slavery. After Douglass recounts Mr. Gore's murder of Demby, he includes several similar stories, such as Mrs. Hick killing her female servant and Beal Bondly killing one of Colonel Lloyd's elderly slaves. These additional scenes serve to support Douglass's claims about slavery. Douglass is attempting to convince white Northerners that the events he witnessed—such as a white man killing a black man and suffering no legal consequences—are the normative practice. Supplementary scenarios reinforce this sense of commonality.

Perhaps the main theme of Douglass's *Narrative* is that slavery dehumanizes men mentally as well as physically. To make this point, Douglass carefully documents the psychological violence of slaveholding. In Chapters III and IV, he focuses on the damaging effects of slaveholders' inconsistency of punishment. He explains how masters often whip slaves when the slaves least deserve it, but neglect to whip them when they most deserve it. Douglass also offers the example of Colonel Lloyd meeting one of his own slaves, unknown to him, in the road. The slave speaks ill of his master, Colonel Lloyd, and is punished for it, but not until several weeks later. This delay of punishment makes the act seem separate from the consequence for the slave. In order to survive, then, slaves must become paranoid and must endure the feeling that they will be punished regardless of their actions.

Once Douglass identifies the mind games that masters play with slaves, he can explain the common actions of slaves as normal human responses under the circumstances. In Chapter III, Douglass addresses some of the less appealing characteristics and actions of slaves, such as prejudice and dishonesty. Douglass explains these actions as natural responses to the slaveholders' treatment of their slaves. He points out that all of these traits are shared by whites and by all humans. Douglass attempts to make his white readers see the slaves as human beings possessed with both reason and emotion—as individuals whose actions are explainable.

When describing the career of the cruel overseer Mr. Gore, Douglass uses an increasingly ironic tone. Irony occurs when the implicit meaning of a statement differs from what is actually asserted. Thus, when Douglass says that Mr. Gore is "what is called a first-rate overseer," he implies that Mr. Gore is a good overseer only to those with no sense of justice. Douglass implies that reasonable people recognize that Mr. Gore is a cruel man. Douglass frequently uses this ironic tone in the *Narrative* to highlight the discrepancy between supposed and actual justice.

CHAPTERS V–VI

SUMMARY: CHAPTER V

Douglass does not work in the fields as a child because children are not strong enough. He has some free time outside his regular tasks. Douglass often accompanies the Colonel's grandson, Daniel, as a servant on hunting expeditions. Daniel eventually becomes attached to Douglass, which is to Douglass's advantage. Douglass still suffers, though. Slave children are given no other clothing but a long linen shirt. The cold of the winters so harms Douglass's feet that he could insert the pen he now writes with into the cracks of his flesh. Children eat corn mush out of a communal trough, so only the strongest children get enough to eat.

At the age of seven or eight, Douglass is selected to go to Baltimore to live with Captain Anthony's son-in-law's brother, Hugh Auld. For three days, Douglass happily prepares to leave Colonel Lloyd's plantation. He cleans himself thoroughly and is rewarded with his first pair of trousers from Lucretia Auld, Captain Anthony's daughter. Douglass is not sad to leave the plantation, as he has no family ties or sense of home, like children usually have. He also feels he has nothing to lose, because even if his new home in Baltimore is full of hardship, it can be no worse than the hardships he has already seen and endured on the plantation. Additionally, Baltimore seems to be a place of promise. Douglass's cousin Tom describes to Douglass the impressive beauty of the city.

Douglass sails on the river to Baltimore on a Saturday morning. He looks once back on Colonel Lloyd's plantation, hoping it will be the last time he sees it. He then sets his sights ahead in the distance. The ship docks at Annapolis first, briefly. Douglass recalls being thoroughly impressed by its size, though in retrospect Annapolis now seems small compared to Northern industrial cities. The ship reaches Baltimore on Sunday morning, and Douglass arrives at his new home. At the Aulds' he is greeted by the kindly face of Mrs. Sophia Auld, her husband, Hugh Auld, and their son, Thomas Auld, who is to be Douglass's master.

Douglass considers his transfer to Baltimore a gift of providence. If he had not been removed from Colonel Lloyd's plantation at that time, Douglass believes he would still be a slave today, rather than a man sitting freely in his home writing his autobiography. Douglass realizes that he may appear superstitious or self-centered to suppose that providence had a hand in his delivery to Baltimore, but the feeling is still strong. From his earliest memory, Douglass recalls sensing that he would not be a slave forever. This sense gives him hope in hard times, and he considers it a gift from God.

Summary: Chapter VI

> *Whilst I was saddened by the thought of losing the aid of my kind mistress, I was gladdened by the invaluable instruction which, by the merest accident, I had gained from my master.*
>
> (See QUOTATIONS, p. 55)

Douglass is astounded by the strange kindness of his new mistress, Sophia Auld. Mrs. Auld has never owned a slave before and seems untouched by the evils of slavery. Douglass is confused by her. Unlike other white women, she does not appreciate his subservience and does not punish him for looking her in the eye. Yet, after some time, the disease of slaveholding overtakes Mrs. Auld too. Her kindness turns to cruelty, and she is utterly changed as a person.

When Douglass first comes to live with the Aulds, Mrs. Auld begins to teach him the alphabet and some small words. When Hugh Auld realizes what she is doing, he orders her to stop immediately, saying that education ruins slaves, making them unmanageable and unhappy. Douglass overhears Mr. Auld and experiences a sudden revelation of the strategy white men use to enslave blacks. He now understands what he must do to win his freedom. Douglass is thankful to Hugh Auld for this enlightenment.

Slaves in the city enjoy relatively greater freedom than plantation slaves. Urban slave owners are careful not to appear cruel or neglectful to slaves in the eyes of non-slaveholding whites. Exceptions to this rule certainly exist, however. The Hamiltons, for example, neighbors of the Aulds, mistreat their two young slaves, Henrietta and Mary. The women's bodies are starved and mangled from Mrs. Hamilton's regular beatings. Douglass himself witnesses Mrs. Hamilton's brutal treatment of the girls.

ANALYSIS: CHAPTERS V–VI

In Chapter V, the *Narrative* returns its focus to Douglass's personal history and away from information or anecdotes about others. Douglass describes his own treatment on Colonel Lloyd's plantation. He is frank about the relative ease of his experience as compared to the adult slaves who worked in the fields. Douglass's candor about the relative lack of hardship he endured as a young slave makes his whole account seem more realistic and truthful. He maintains this frank and moderate tone throughout the *Narrative*.

Douglass uses a striking image to describe the frostbite wounds he suffered as a child, as it dramatizes his doubleness of self. He describes how the pen with which he is now writing could fit inside the cracks on his foot he suffered from the cold. In the *Narrative,* Douglass typically maintains a dichotomy between his free, educated, literate self—which does not appear as a body—and the abused body of his unenlightened slave self. In his image of the pen in the gash, however, Douglass momentarily collapses the distance between his two selves, suggesting that the distinction between the two is not always clear.

Douglass's relocation to Baltimore is the first major change in his life, and the shift of setting introduces the notion of the greater freedom of cities versus the countryside. Cities—and especially Northern cities—in the *Narrative* offer enlightenment, prosperity, and a degree of social freedom. Only in cities is Douglass able to connect with different kinds of people and new intellectual ideas. By contrast, the countryside appears in the *Narrative* as a place of extremely limited freedom. In rural areas, slaves have less mobility and are more closely watched by slave owners. This motif contributes to the movement of the *Narrative*: Douglass is symbolically closest to Northern freedom when in the city of Baltimore, and is symbolically furthest from freedom when in rural areas.

While Douglass's *Narrative* shows that slavery dehumanizes slaves, it also advances the idea that slavery adversely affects slave owners. Douglass makes this point in previous chapters by showing the damaging self-deceptions that slave owners must construct to keep their minds at ease. These self-deceptions build upon one another until slave owners are left without religion or reason, with hypocrisy as the basis of their existence. Douglass uses the figure of Sophia Auld to illustrate this process. When Douglass arrives to live with Hugh and Sophia Auld, Sophia treats Douglass as nearly an equal to her own son. Soon, however, Hugh schools Sophia in the ways of slavery, teaching her the immoral slave-master relationship that gives one individual complete power over another. Douglass depicts Sophia's transformation in horrific terms. She seems to lose all human qualities and to become an evil, inhuman being. Douglass presents Sophia as much a victim of the institution of slavery as Douglass himself is.

The fact that Sophia is a woman helps Douglass's portrayal of her as a victim of slavery. It is significant that the male slaveholders of Douglass's *Narrative*, even Hugh Auld, all appear to be already schooled in the vice of slavery. Women, and Sophia especially, exist in Douglass's *Narrative* as idealistically sympathetic and virtuous beings—a gender stereotype common in nineteenth-century culture. Thus Sophia becomes, along with the slaves themselves, an object of sympathy for Douglass's readers. The readers' horror and regret for Sophia's lost kindness reinforces their sense that slavery is unnatural and evil.

The first pivotal moment in Douglass's mental life is in Chapter I, when he is initiated into the horrors of slavery by seeing Captain Anthony whip Aunt Hester. The second turning point in Douglass's youth occurs when Hugh Auld refuses to allow Douglass to become educated. Before this moment, Douglass has known intuitively that slavery is evil, but has been mystified by the logic of how slavery works. Hugh Auld's pronouncement that education ruins slaves enlightens Douglass. He suddenly understands that slave owners gain and keep power over slaves by depriving slaves of education and ideas. Douglass realizes that he must become educated to become free. The idea that education is the means to freedom is a major theme in the *Narrative*.

Douglass presents his revelation about the importance of education as a moment of both alignment with and opposition to Hugh Auld. Though it is Sophia Auld who has been teaching Douglass to read, Douglass values Hugh Auld's lesson more. Douglass presents the moment as a rejection of feminine lessons in favor of masculine authoritative knowledge. Douglass further aligns himself with Hugh Auld by pledging to place himself in opposition to Auld. A series of rhetorical antitheses pair the two, such as "What [Hugh Auld] most loved, that I most hated." Throughout the *Narrative*, Douglass's progress rests on this focus on white male authority.

CHAPTERS VII–VIII

SUMMARY: CHAPTER VII

Douglass lives in Hugh Auld's household for about seven years. During this time, he is able to learn how to read and write, though Mrs. Auld is hardened and no longer tutors him. Slavery hurts Mrs. Auld as much as it hurts Douglass himself. The mentality of slavery strips her of her inherent piety and sympathy for others, making her hardened and cruel.

However, Douglass has already learned the alphabet and is determined to learn how to read. He gives bread to poor local boys in exchange for reading lessons. Douglass writes that he is now tempted to thank these boys by name, but he knows that they would suffer for it, as teaching blacks still constitutes an offense. Douglass recalls the boys sympathetically agreeing that he no more deserved to be a slave than they did themselves.

At around the age of twelve, Douglass encounters a book called *The Columbian Orator*, which contains a philosophical dialogue between a master and a slave. In the dialogue, the master lays out the argument for slavery, and the slave refutes each point, eventually convincing the master to release him. The book also contains a reprint of a speech arguing for the emancipation of Irish Catholics and for human rights generally. The book helps Douglass to fully articulate the case against slavery, but it also makes him hate his masters more and more. This dilemma is difficult position for Douglass and often fills him with regret. As Hugh Auld predicted, Douglass's discontent is painfully acute now that he understands the injustice of his situation but still has no means by which to escape it. Douglass enters a period of nearly suicidal despair.

During this period, Douglass eagerly listens to anyone discussing slavery. He often hears the word "abolitionist." In a city newspaper account of a Northern abolitionist petition, Douglass finally discovers that the word means "antislavery."

One day around this time, Douglass kindly helps two Irish sailors at the wharf without being asked. When they realize that Douglass is doomed to be a slave for life, the sailors encourage him to run away to the North. Douglass does not respond to them, for fear they might be trying to trick him. White men are known to encourage slaves to escape and then recapture them for the reward money. But the idea of escape nonetheless sticks in Douglass's head.

Meanwhile, Douglass sets out to learn how to write. After watching ships' carpenters write single letters on lumber, Douglass learns to form several letters. He practices his letters on fences, walls, and the ground around the city. He approaches local boys and starts contests over who can write the best. Douglass writes what he can and learns from what the boys write. Soon, he can copy from the dictionary. When the Aulds leave Douglass alone in the house, he writes in Thomas Auld's old discarded copybooks. In this painstaking manner, Douglass eventually learns to write.

SUMMARY: CHAPTER VIII

During Douglass's first several years in Baltimore, his old master, Captain Anthony, dies. When Douglass is between ten and eleven years old, he is returned to the plantation to be appraised among the other slaves and the livestock, which are to be divided between Captain Anthony's surviving children, Mrs. Lucretia Auld and Andrew Anthony. Douglass is apprehensive about leaving Baltimore because he knows his life in the city is preferable to the plantation.

The valuation of the slaves is humiliating, as they are inspected alongside the livestock. All the slaves are anxious, knowing they are to be divided regardless of marriages, family, and friendships. Master Andrew is known for his cruelty and drunkenness, so everyone hopes to avoid becoming his property. Since Douglass's return to the plantation, he has seen Master Andrew kick Douglass's younger brother in the head until he bled. Master Andrew has threatened to do the same to Douglass.

Luckily, Douglass is assigned to Mrs. Lucretia Auld, who sends him back to Baltimore. Soon after Douglass returns there, Mrs. Lucretia and Master Andrew both die, leaving all the Anthony family property in the hands of strangers. Neither Lucretia nor

Andrew frees any of the slaves before dying—not even Douglass's grandmother, who nurtured Master Andrew from infancy to death. Because Douglass's grandmother is deemed too old to work in the fields, her new owners abandon her in a small hut in the woods. Douglass bemoans this cruel fate. He imagines that if his grandmother were still alive today, she would be cold and lonely, mourning the loss of her children.

About two years after the death of Lucretia Auld, her husband, Thomas Auld, remarries. Soon after the marriage, Thomas has a falling out with his brother, Hugh, and punishes Hugh by reclaiming Douglass. Douglass is not sorry to leave Hugh and Sophia Auld, as Hugh has become a drunk and Sophia has become cruel. But Douglass is sorry to leave the local boys, who have become his friends and teachers.

While sailing from Baltimore back to the Eastern Shore of Maryland, Douglass pays particular attention to the route of the ships heading north to Philadelphia. He resolves to escape at the earliest opportunity.

ANALYSIS: CHAPTERS VII–VIII

In Chapters VII and VIII, Douglass relates events slightly out of chronological order, again disrupting the *Narrative*'s appearance of autobiography. His brief return to the plantation, recounted in Chapter VIII, actually takes place before he reads *The Colombian Orator*, recounted in Chapter VII. Douglass records the events out of order because he favors thematic consistency over strict chronology. As Chapter VI deals with Hugh Auld forbidding Sophia to teach Douglass to read, Chapter VII addresses Douglass's self-education and the fulfillment of Hugh Auld's predictions of unhappiness.

Chapter VII elaborates the idea that with education comes enlightenment—specifically, enlightenment about the oppressive and wrong nature of slavery. Douglass's reading lessons and acts of reading are, therefore, contiguous with his growing understanding of the social injustice of slavery. Douglass gets his first reading lessons from neighborhood boys and also engages in discussions about the institution of slavery with them. These boys not only provide the means of Douglass's education, but also support his growing political convictions. In this way, Douglass depicts each step in his educational process as a simultaneous step in philosophical and political enlightenment.

Douglass's encounter with *The Columbian Orator* represents the main event of Douglass's educational and philosophical growth. This book features both a Socratic-style dialogue between an archetypal "master" and "slave" and a speech in favor of Irish Catholic emancipation. Douglass has a sense of the inhumanity of slavery before he reads *The Columbian Orator,* but the book gives him a clear articulation of the political and philosophical argument against slavery and in favor of human rights. It allows Douglass to formulate his personal thoughts and convictions about slavery. However, the book also causes Douglass to detest his masters. Painfully, he understands the injustice of his position, but has no immediate means of escape. In this regard, Douglass fulfills Hugh Auld's prediction that educated slaves become unhappy. Douglass's unhappiness shows that education does not directly bring freedom. His new consciousness of injustice has drawbacks, and intellectual freedom is not the same as physical freedom.

Chapters VII and VIII further develop the *Narrative*'s motif of the greater freedom of the city compared to the countryside. Chapter VII takes place in Baltimore and features Douglass's free movements and self-education. Douglass hardly discusses the Aulds or their cruel treatment in Chapter VII. Instead, he focuses on his intellectually fruitful interactions with people around the city, such as neighborhood boys and dock workers. Chapter VIII, however, deals with Douglass's time in the countryside. First, Douglass discusses his brief trip back to the Eastern Shore around age ten and then his return to Thomas Auld's plantation three years later. These disparate historical events are out of chronological order with the events of Chapter VII. They are united in one chapter because of their common rural setting. Douglass portrays the oppressive atmosphere of the rural plantation, where slaves are closely watched, harshly punished, and treated as property.

In Chapter VIII, Douglass elaborates on the idea of slave owners treating slaves as property through his depiction of the valuation of Captain Anthony's slaves. Douglass ironically describes how Captain Anthony's slaves are lined up alongside the livestock to be valued in the same manner. Douglass's irony points to the absurdity of treating humans as animals. Douglass further develops this idea by showing how slaves are frequently passed from owner to owner as property. In Chapter VIII alone, Douglass is under the ownership of Captain Anthony, then Lucretia and Thomas Auld, then Hugh Auld, and then Thomas Auld once again. Douglass's extended description of the Anthony family's treatment of his grandmother particularly develops this motif of ownership. Though Douglass's grandmother lovingly tends the Anthony children for her entire life, they do not grant her freedom even in her old age. Because slave owners value slaves only according to the amount labor they can do, Douglass's grandmother's new owners abandon the elderly woman.

Several times in his *Narrative,* Douglass breaks the conventions of his past-tense autobiography to recreate a scene imaginatively. In his discussion of the treatment of his grandmother, Douglass imagines that she is still alive as he is writing. He creates an image of her stumbling around her small hut, waiting for death. This imagined scene works in the same ways as sentimental fiction. Douglass evokes the conventional scene of the home hearth surrounded by happy children to contrast it with the desolation of his grandmother's life. Douglass's grandmother becomes an object of sympathy—a sympathy meant to translate into outrage and political conviction.

Chapters IX–X

Summary: Chapter IX

Douglass arrives to live at Thomas Auld's in March 1832. Life under Auld is particularly difficult because Auld does not give the slaves enough food. Douglass works in the kitchen alongside his sister, Eliza; his aunt, Priscilla; and another woman, Henny. They have to beg or steal food from neighbors to survive, though the Aulds always seem to have food wasting in the storehouse.

As a slave owner, Thomas Auld has absolutely no redeeming qualities. His meanness is in accord with the fact that he was not born with slaves, but acquired them through marriage. Douglass reports that adoptive slaveholders are notoriously the worst masters. Auld is inconsistent in his discipline and cowardly in his cruelty. In August 1832, Auld attends a Methodist camp meeting and suddenly becomes quite religious—and even more cruel. Some of the religious figures in the community, however, act kindly to slaves. One man named Mr. Wilson even runs a slave school until the community shuts it down. Auld, on the other hand, only uses his new-found piety to justify his cruelty to his slaves with added fervor.

While Douglass lives under Auld, he sometimes purposely lets Auld's horse run away to a nearby farm. Douglass then goes to fetch the horse and eats a full meal at the neighboring farm. After this happens several times, Auld decides to rent Douglass to Edward Covey for one year. Covey is a poor man with a reputation for successfully taming problem slaves. Slave owners give Covey their slaves for one year, during which he "breaks" the slaves while using them as free labor on his land. Douglass knows of Covey's sinister reputation, but looks forward to being fed sufficiently at Covey's.

SUMMARY: CHAPTER X

From the beginning of Chapter X through Douglass's fight with Covey

Douglass arrives at Covey's farm on January 1, 1833, and he is forced to work in the fields for the first time. His first task is to guide a team of unbroken oxen. The oxen are uncooperative, and Douglass barely escapes with his life. Finding that Douglass has failed, Covey orders him to take off his clothes and receive punishment. When Douglass does not respond, Covey rushes at him, tears his clothing off, and whips him repeatedly. Covey continues to whip Douglass almost weekly, usually as punishment for Douglass's supposed "awkwardness."

Covey's slaves must work in the fields during all the daylight hours, with few breaks for meals. Unlike most slave owners, Covey often works in the fields with his slaves. He also has a habit of sneaking up on the slaves by crawling through the cornfield in an attempt to catch them resting. Because of this behavior, the slaves call him "the snake."

Covey behaves deceitfully even in regard to his religion. His excessive piety seems designed to convince himself that he is a faithful man, even though he is guilty of blatant sins such as adultery. Covey owns one slave named Caroline whom he bought to be a "breeder." Covey has hired a married man to sleep with Caroline every night so that she will produce more slaves for Covey to own.

Douglass recalls that he spent his hardest times as a slave during his first six months rented to Covey. Douglass becomes deadened by work, exhaustion, and Covey's repeated punishments. Douglass loses his spirit, his intellect, his desire to learn, and his natural cheerfulness. Sunday is the slaves' only leisure time, and Douglass usually spends the day in a stupor in the shade. He considers killing himself, or even Covey, but he is paralyzed by both hope and fear.

Covey's house is situated near the banks of the Chesapeake Bay, where large ships with white sails travel past. To Douglass, these ships symbolize freedom, cruelly reminding him of his own enslaved condition. Douglass recalls standing on the bank and speaking aloud to the ships, asking them why they should be free and he enslaved. He begs for God's deliverance and then wonders if there actually is a God. He vows to run away.

Having traced his dehumanization from a man into a slave, Douglass now recounts his transformation back into a man. In August 1833, on a particularly hot day, Douglass collapses from fatigue. Covey discovers him and kicks and hits him with a plank. Douglass resolves to return to Thomas Auld and complain about Covey. When Covey is not looking, Douglass starts to walk feebly to Auld's. Douglass has blood pouring from his head and his progress is slow. He stays in the woods to avoid detection. Douglass finally arrives at Auld's and complains about Covey's behavior. At first Auld seems sympathetic, but then he insists that Douglass return to Covey's.

When Douglass arrives back at Covey's the next morning, Covey runs toward him with a whip. Douglass runs and hides in the cornfield among the stalks. Covey eventually gives up searching for him and leaves. Douglass returns to the woods, where he runs into Sandy Jenkins, a slave from a neighboring farm. Sandy is traveling to the home of his free wife, and he invites Douglass to come. At the house, Douglass explains his troubles to Sandy. Sandy advises Douglass to carry a certain magical root from the woods, explaining that the root will save him from white men's beatings. Douglass is skeptical, but then decides it cannot hurt to try.

Douglass returns to Covey's on Sunday morning with the root in hand. Covey, who is on his way to a religious meeting, speaks kindly to Douglass. Douglass begins to suspect that the root has worked. But on Monday morning, Covey finds Douglass in the stable and attempts to tie his legs. Douglass suddenly decides to fight back. He grabs Covey by the throat in an effort to keep Covey from tying and whipping him. Covey is terrified and calls for another slave, Hughes, to hold Douglass back. Hughes approaches, and Douglass kicks him down. Next, Covey calls on another slave, Bill, for aid, but Bill refuses. Douglass explains to Covey that he will not stand being treated like an animal any longer. The two men fight for two hours. Covey brags afterward that he whipped Douglass, but he did not. Covey never touches Douglass again.

[T]he dark night of slavery closed in upon me; and
behold a man transformed into a brute!

(See QUOTATIONS, p. 56)

ANALYSIS: CHAPTERS IX–X

In Chapter IX, Douglass uses the character of Thomas Auld to show that slaveholding is not a natural way of life. Because Auld was not born owning slaves, he must learn the techniques of being a slave master. Auld imitates the mannerisms of someone comfortable with power, but he is unsuccessful in his imitation. Both the slaves and Auld himself realize the falseness of his manner, and Auld becomes more cruel to compensate for his own inconsistency. Douglass shows that the power of slaveholders is created through role-playing. Auld fails as a slaveholder because his role-playing is unskilled. If power, then, consists only of the successful enactment of outward demeanor, actions, and words, it follows that slaveholding must not be part of the natural order.

Auld also serves as a vehicle for one of Douglass's main themes in the *Narrative*—the dangerous alliance between slaveholders and false Christianity. Douglass recounts Auld's religious conversion and notes that Auld's cruelty increases after the conversion. Auld, like many others, creates an image of himself as an upstanding Christian. He uses this self-image to justify his actions toward his slaves. In turn, the church community benefits from Auld's slaveholding wealth. Douglass is careful to point out that one or two members of Auld's Christian community are truly religious people who display sympathy for the slaves. Thus Douglass sets up a dichotomy between "true" and "false" Christianity.

Douglass also presents Edward Covey as an example of a slave owner perverting Christianity. Covey considers himself a pious man, yet he has forced a female slave into adultery with a married man. With Covey, Douglass shows that this false Christianity can be a symptom of the negative effects of slaveholding on slave owners. Because of the evils Covey perpetrates against his slaves, he must deceive himself with elaborate displays of piety in order to preserve his sense of moral righteousness. Douglass presents this self-deception as a damaging way of life.

Douglass also points to the falseness of Covey's Christianity by drawing parallels between Covey and Satan. The slaves refer to Covey as "the snake"—a nickname that is a clear reference to Satan in the Garden of Eden from the biblical story of Genesis. Covey's cunning and deceitfulness further align him with the figure of Satan, undermining his professions of piety.

In Chapter X, Douglass's *Narrative* clearly fits the conventions of several types of autobiography—the "underdog" story, the success story, and the religious conversion narrative. These subgenres usually portray the decline of the protagonist's fortunes, followed by a climactic turning point in which the protagonist has some sort of revelation. The *Narrative* shows Douglass's decline during his first six months with Covey, and at the end of this time, Douglass's spirits are lower than ever. Douglass then presents his fight with Covey as the turning point in his life. Douglass highlights this moment as the climax of the *Narrative* by using a rhetorical phrase that hinges on a reversal of fortune: "You have seen how a man was made a slave; you shall see how a slave was made a man."

Douglass is vague about the role that Sandy's magical root plays in his successful battle with Covey. Sandy's root seems to symbolize a kind of religion different from Douglass's own spiritual Christianity. Douglass associates the root with backward ideas—and possibly traditional African ideas. Douglass does not go so far as to say that the root has no effect, though, and he admits to having wondered about it. Douglass's conflicted attitude toward the root arises again in Chapter XI. In a footnote, Douglass identifies Sandy as "superstitious," attributing beliefs similar to Sandy's belief in the root to "ignorant" slaves. Douglass's authority in the *Narrative* relies on the distance between his writing self and his slave self, and the distance between himself and unenlightened slaves. Therefore, Douglass must ultimately dismiss the root as having no power.

Though the *Narrative* treats knowledge as the means to freedom, Douglass presents his transformation from slave to free man as an act of violence. Douglass regains his personal spirit, interest in learning, and conviction to be free by physically fighting against his oppressor, Covey. Yet Douglass's violence takes the form of controlled violence or self-defense. He does not advocate vengeance, but rather controlled confrontation. Through this contained aggression, Douglass asserts himself and achieves his larger goal—to end physical violence between Covey and himself.

CHAPTER X (CONTINUED)

From Douglass's fight with Covey through end of Chapter X

SUMMARY

> *In coming to a fixed determination to run away, we*
> *did more than Patrick Henry, when he resolved upon*
> *liberty or death.*
>
> (See QUOTATIONS, p. 57)

The fight with Covey causes Douglass to regain his spirit and defiance, as well as his resolve to be free. He never receieves a whipping from anyone during his remaining four years as a slave. Douglass's year with Covey ends on Christmas Day, 1833. It is customary for slaves to enjoy a holiday from Christmas to New Year's. Slaveholders typically encourage slaves to spend the holiday drinking, rather than resting or working industriously for themselves. Douglass explains that this strategy helps keep blacks enslaved. By giving slaves a brief span of time each year to release their rebellious spirit, slaveholders keep them manageable for the rest of the year. By encouraging them to spend the holiday riotously drunk, slaveholders ensure that freedom comes to seem unappealing.

On January 1, 1834, Douglass is sent to live with Mr. William Freeland. Mr. Freeland, though quick-tempered, is more consistently fair than Covey. Douglass is grateful that Mr. Freeland is not a hypocritically religious man. Many men in the community profess to be religious, but merely use their religion as justification for their cruelty to their slaves.

Freeland works his slaves hard, but treats them fairly. Douglass meets and befriends other slaves on Freeland's property, including the intelligent brothers Henry and John Harris. Sandy Jenkins also lives at Freeland's at this time, and Douglass reminds readers about Sandy's root and reports that Sandy's superstition is common among the more ignorant slaves.

Douglass soon succeeds in getting some of his fellow slaves interested in learning how to read. Word soon spreads, and Douglass surreptitiously begins to hold a Sabbath school in the cabin of a free black. This is a dangerous undertaking, as educating slaves is forbidden; the community violently shuts down a similar school run by a white man. Yet the slaves value their education so highly that they attend Douglass's school despite the threat of punishment.

Douglass's first year with Freeland passes smoothly. Douglass remembers Freeland as the best master he ever had. Douglass also attributes the comfort of the year to his solidarity with the other slaves. Douglass recalls that he loved them and that they operated together as a single community.

Though Douglass remains with Freeland for another year in 1835, by this time he desires his freedom more strongly than ever. Here Douglass puns on the comfort of living with "Freeland" as his master and his stronger desire to live on "free land." Douglass, resolving to attempt an escape sometime during the year, sets about offering his fellow slaves the chance to join him. Douglass recalls how daunting the odds were for them. He describes their position as facing the bloody figure of slavery and glimpsing the doubtful, beckoning figure of freedom in the distance, with the intervening path full of hardship and death. Douglass points out that their decision was far more difficult than that of Patrick Henry, whose choice between death and an oppressed life—"Give me liberty or give me death"—was merely rhetorical. As slaves, Douglass and his companions had to choose doubtful liberty over nearly certain death.

The escape party consists of Douglass, Henry and John Harris, Henry Bailey, and Charles Roberts. Sandy Jenkins initially intends to accompany them, but eventually decides to remain. They plan to canoe up the Chesapeake Bay on the Saturday before Easter. Douglass writes travel passes, signed by their master, for each of them.

On the morning of their planned escape, Douglass works in the fields as usual. He soon feels overcome by a sense that their plan has been betrayed. Douglass tells Sandy Jenkins of his fear, and Sandy feels the same way. During breakfast, William Hamilton and several other men arrive at the house. They seize and tie Douglass and the rest of the escape party. The men transport their prisoners to Thomas Auld's house. On the way, Douglass and the others speak together, agreeing to destroy their written passes and admit nothing.

At Thomas Auld's, Douglass and the others learn that someone has betrayed them. Douglass writes that they immediately knew who the betrayer was, but he does not reveal who they suspected. The men are placed in jail. Slave traders arrive to taunt them and size them up as though to sell them. At the end of the Easter holidays, all the slaves but Douglass are taken home. Douglass remains in jail because he is identified as the leader and instigator. He begins to despair. At first, Thomas Auld announces his intent to send Douglass to Alabama. Then Auld suddenly changes his mind and sends Douglass back to Baltimore with Hugh Auld.

In Baltimore, Hugh Auld apprentices Douglass to a shipbuilder named William Gardner. Douglass is to learn the trade of ship caulking. Because Gardner's shipyard is struggling to meet a deadline, however, Douglass becomes a helping hand for seventy-five different carpenters and learns no new skill. The carpenters constantly summon and yell at Douglass, who cannot help them all at once. Tensions at the shipyard increase when the white carpenters suddenly strike to protest the free black carpenters who Gardner has hired. Gardner agrees to fire the free black carpenters. As an apprentice who is not free, Douglass continues working at Gardner's, but he endures severe physical intimidation from the white apprentices.

One day, four white apprentices attack Douglass at the shipyard and nearly destroy his left eye. He starts to fight back but decides against it, as lynch law dictates that any black man who hits a white man may be killed. Instead, Douglass complains to Hugh Auld, who becomes surprisingly indignant on Douglass's behalf. Auld takes Douglass with him to see a lawyer, but the lawyer informs them that no warrant may be issued without the testimony of a white man.

Douglass spends time at home recovering, and later he becomes an apprentice at Hugh Auld's own shipyard. Douglass quickly learns caulking under Walter Price and soon earns the highest possible wage. Each week, Douglass turns over all his wages to Hugh Auld. Douglass compares Auld to a pirate who has a "right" to Douglass's wages only because he has the power to compel Douglass to hand them over.

ANALYSIS

The second half of Chapter X continues to shift between personal accounts and public arguments against slavery. Douglass moves from the personal account of the rest of the year under Covey to a general analysis of the "holiday" that slave owners give their slaves between Christmas and New Year's. Generally, the public, or persuasive—sections of the *Narrative* generally either disprove pro-slavery arguments, present antislavery arguments, or disabuse readers of misinformation or misinterpretation about the practices of slave owners. Douglass's analysis of the holiday time falls in this last category. To the uninformed observer, it would appear a positive thing that slave owners grant a holiday to their slaves. Douglass explains, however, that this seeming benevolence is part of the larger power structure of slavery. Slaveholders use holiday time to make their slaves disaffected with "freedom" and to keep them from revolting.

The figure of William Freeland stands in direct contrast to the rest of the slave owners in Douglass's *Narrative*. Douglass's previous masters have all shared one or both of two traits: hypocritical piety or inconsistent brutality. Douglass presents Freeland as a good slave owner because he lacks both of these vices. Freeland has no pretensions about religion and is consistent and fair in his treatment of his slaves. However, though Freeland is a good model for a slave owner, Douglass remains clear that slaveholding in any form is still unjust. He points to his dissatisfaction with Freeland in a pun on Freeland's name. Instead of equating "Freeland" with "free land," Douglass uses the pun to point out that belonging to "Freeland" is not as good a guarantee as living on "free land."

Douglass's experience under Freeland is also positive because he develops a social network of fellow slaves that during this time. Except for his friendship with the local boys in Baltimore, Douglass has been a figure of isolation and alienation in the *Narrative*. As an isolated figure, he appropriately resembles the protagonist of a traditional coming-of-age story. These autobiographical stories tend to privilege a model of heroic individualism over social interaction and support. In Chapter X, however, Douglass reveals the close friendships he develops at Freeland's and shows that he relies on friends' support. This model of social support competes with the model of heroic individualism through the end of Douglass's *Narrative*. For example, Douglass's first escape attempt involves several people and fails, whereas he presents his successful escape as the act of an individual.

In their prefaces to Douglass's *Narrative*, Garrison and Phillips place Douglass in the context of the American Revolutionaries' battle for rights and freedom. Douglass himself uses this context in Chapter X when he specifies that escaping slaves act more bravely than Patrick Henry did. Douglass alludes to Henry's famous declaration, "Give me liberty or give me death." While Henry faces a choice between political independence and oppression, escaping slaves must choose between two unattractive options—the familiar ills of slavery and the unknown dangers of escape. While Garrison and Phillips make a direct connection between Douglass and the

Revolutionaries, Douglass uses a reference to the Revolutionaries to highlight the differences between the plight of slaves and the glamour of the Revolutionaries' battle for rights.

For Douglass, the difference between the Revolutionaries and slaves is widened by the fact that slaves do not benefit from the citizen's rights for which the Revolutionaries fought. When four of Gardner's white apprentices attack Douglass, Douglass enjoys neither the right to defend himself nor the right see his attackers punished for their crime. Douglass ironically portrays his master Hugh Auld as naïvely surprised and indignant upon hearing the lawyer say that a slave has no right to stand witness against a white. The irony with which Douglass writes of American "human rights" in theory and in practice also seems present in the *Narrative*'s subtitle, *An American Slave*. The *Narrative* goes on to show that the words "American" and "slave" are contradictory: the rights afforded by the designation "American" are nonexistent for slaves.

In Chapter X we see Douglass working for wages for the first time. Previously, his labor translated into invisible profit for his masters, but when he begins apprenticing at shipyards, he begins to receive the monetary value of his labor. Douglass must must turn over these wages to Hugh Auld each week, however. The physical presence of the money Douglass earns with his labor reinforces his sense of the injustice of slavery. Hugh Auld comes to resemble a thief who steals what is not his, rather than an owner of property by which he profits.

Chapter XI & Appendix

Summary: Chapter XI
Douglass explains that the final chapter of his *Narrative* portrays the part of his life during which he escaped from slavery. He explains, however, that the chapter does not describe the exact means of his escape, as he does not want to give slaveholders any information that would help them prevent other slaves from escaping to the North. In fact, Douglass hopes slaveholders will become frantic with thoughts of unseen foes around them, ready to snatch their slaves away from them or hinder them in their quest to reclaim their slaves.

Douglass resumes his narrative in the spring of 1838, when he begins to object to turning over all his wages to Hugh Auld. Auld sometimes gives Douglass a small portion of the wages, which only confirms Douglass's feeling that he is entitled to the wages in their entirety. Auld appears to sense this unfairness and tries to remedy his guilt by giving Douglass small portions of the money.

Thomas Auld visits Baltimore, and Douglass approaches him asking to be allowed to seek work on his own. Thomas Auld refuses him, assuming that Douglass intends to escape. Two months later, Douglass asks the same of Hugh Auld, who agrees, with the stipulation that Douglass must find all his own work and pay Auld three dollars each week to buy his own tools, board, and clothing. Though it is an ungenerous arrangement, Douglass looks forward to having the responsibilities of a free man.

For four months, Douglass hires his own time and pays Hugh Auld on Saturdays. Then, one Saturday in August, Douglass gets delayed at a meeting outside Baltimore and is unable to give Auld his wages until the next day. Hugh Auld is furious and revokes Douglass's privilege of hiring his own time, fearing that Douglass will soon attempt to escape. In protest, Douglass does no work the following week, to Auld's anger and dismay. Then Douglass resolves to escape on the third of September. He decides to work diligently until that date to keep Auld from growing suspicious.

As the date of escape draws closer, Douglass experiences anxiety about leaving his many Baltimore friends and about the possibility of failure. Nonetheless, he carries his plan through and reaches New York City smoothly on the third of September. Rather than feeling relieved upon reaching New York, however, Douglass is seized with terror. He finds himself in an unfamiliar city, without shelter, food, money, or friends. He is surrounded by people, but afraid to speak with anyone for fear they will turn him in. Soon, though, a free black named David Ruggles takes Douglass in. Ruggles, an abolitionist and journalist, advises Douglass to go to New Bedford, Massachusetts, to find work as a caulker. Douglass writes to his fiancée, Anna Murray, a free black woman from Baltimore. Anna joins Douglass in New York. Ruggles witnesses their marriage and gives Douglass five dollars and a letter of recommendation.

When Douglass and Anna reach New Bedford, they receive help from Mr. and Mrs. Nathan Johnson, who pay their travel debt and help Douglass choose a new name. Mr. Johnson suggests "Douglass," the name of a knight in Sir Walter Scott's *Lady of the Lake.*

Douglass is surprised by the wealthy and clean appearance of New Bedford. Douglass has always assumed that Northerners, because they own no slaves, are poor. But the city's industries appear prosperous, and the workers labor smoothly. Douglass sees no extreme poverty. Even the city's blacks enjoy good living conditions. They are more politically aware and educated than many Southern slaveholders. Additionally, the Northern blacks take care of one another and guard escaped slaves from recapture.

Douglass works for the next three years in miscellaneous jobs at the docks in New Bedford. After several months, he earns enough money to subscribe to the *Liberator,* an abolitionist magazine. In August 1841, Douglass attends an antislavery convention in Nantucket and is urged to speak about his experience as a slave. He is nervous about speaking in front of whites, but soon talks with ease. Since that day, Douglass has worked to plead the case against slavery.

Summary: Appendix

Douglass uses the appendix to clarify his position about religion. He concontends that there is a great gap between the pure and peaceful Christianity of Christ and the corrupt Christianity of slaveholding America. Douglass articulates his understanding of the hypocrisy of Southern "Christians" who whip slaves, prostitute female slaves, and steal the wages of working slaves while professing Christian values of humility, purity, and virtue. Douglass implies that the Southern church and slaveholders support each other. The church accepts the slave money of slaveholders. Douglass quotes from the Bible, an abolitionist poem, and a parodic version of a Southern hymn to support his argument.

Analysis: Chapter XI & Appendix

Douglass's explanation about why he does not describe the means of his escape elaborates on one of the *Narrative's* main themes—the perpetuation of slavery through enforced ignorance. Douglass has said that slave owners keep blacks enslaved by refusing to let them be educated. Douglass presents this strategy as an aggressive, dehumanizing policy. In Chapter XI, Douglass turns the tables, refusing to educate slaveholders about the means of his escape or about how slaves escape in general. Douglass does not want slaveholders and slave catchers to stop slaves from escaping in the future. But Douglass's tone also becomes impassioned, as he suggests that he also wishes that slaveholders and slavecatchers suffer in their ignorance. Just as ignorance dehumanizes slaves, Douglass imagines that ignorance about slaves' means of escape will change slaveholders into hunted animals. The slaveholders' panic and paranoia would be comparable to what slaves are made to feel. Douglass's tone makes this wish seem vindictive, but it also expands a theme of the *Narrative,* showing that lack of knowledge robs people of their ability to control.

The second, implicit, reason that Douglass does not relay the details of his escape to the North is to protect the safety of those who helped him. Douglass's account of the time of his escape is understandably conflicted as a result. Douglass acknowledges that he has friends and a fiancée in Baltimore, but he does not provide any information about his relationships with them. The only indication of how important Douglass's friends are to him is the extent to which he suffers from their absence in New York City. This omission of supportive characters from the *Narrative* seems to be not only an effort to protect their identities, but also a concession to the conventions of the individual success story. The *Narrative* suggests that slaves are made on an individual level by depriving men of selfhood. The *Narrative* therefore shows Douglass's quest for freedom as an individual accomplishment, achieved without the help of others.

Douglass's first few days alone in New York represent a new stage in his self-formation. Douglass renders this time as a new sort of trial—a trial of solitude—and his rhetorical treatment of this time reinforces his feelings of isolation. Douglass gives the reader a sense of his circumstances and sentiments at this time, but he also repeatedly insists that no reader can fully sympathize with his feelings without experiencing all of the conditions he himself faced. Douglass's rhetoric invites the reader to imagine his feelings while forcing the reader to recognize the impossibility of this imagining. The passage thus sets apart Douglass's first few days in New York as a difficult, individual trial.

IMPORTANT QUOTATIONS EXPLAINED

1. Never having enjoyed, to any considerable extent, her soothing presence, her tender and watchful care, I received the tidings of [my mother's] death with much the same emotions I should have probably felt at the death of a stranger.

In this passage, which appears in Chapter I of the *Narrative*, Douglass explains that his master separated him from his mother soon after his birth. This separation ensured that Douglass did not develop familial feelings toward his mother. Douglass devotes large parts of his *Narrative* to demonstrating how a slave is "made," beginning at birth. To some readers in Douglass's time it may have seemed natural for blacks to be kept as slaves. Douglass upsets this point of view by depicting the unnaturalness of slavery. He explains the means by which slave owners distort social bonds and the natural processes of life in order to turn men into slaves. This process begins at birth, as Douglass shows in Chapter I, which describes his introduction into slavery. Slaveholders first remove a child from his immediate family, and Douglass explains how this destroys the child's support network and sense of personal history.

In this quotation, Douglass uses descriptive adjectives like "soothing" and "tender" to re-create imaginatively the childhood he would have known if his mother had been present. Douglass often exercises this imaginative recreation in his *Narrative* in order to contrast normal stages of childhood development with the quality of development that he knew as a child. This comparative presentation creates a strong sense of disparity between the two and underscores the injustice that creates that disparity.

Though Douglass's style in this passage is dry and restrained, his focus on the family structure and the woeful moment of his mother's death is typical of the conventions of nineteenth-century sentimental narratives. Nineteenth-century readers placed great value on the family structure, viewing families as a haven of virtue. The destruction of family structure would have saddened readers and appeared to be a signal of the larger moral illnesses of the culture. Douglass, like many nineteenth-century authors, shows how social injustice can be expressed through the breakdown of a family structure.

2.   I did not, when a slave, understand the deep meaning
       of those rude and apparently incoherent songs. I was
       myself within the circle; so that I neither saw nor
       heard as those without might see and hear.

This passage is part of Douglass's long discussion at the end of Chapter II about the songs that slaves sing. As he often does in the *Narrative,* Douglass takes his personal experience of hearing slaves sing on their way to the Great House Farm and analyzes this as a common experience among all slaves. He uses his conclusions about slave behavior to correct white readers' misconceptions. In this instance, Douglass explains that many Northerners mistakenly believe that the singing of slaves is evidence of their happiness. He says that the songs are actually evidence, on an almost subconscious emotional level, of the slaves' deep unhappiness.

In this discussion, Douglass makes a distinction between the literal and the "deep" meaning of the songs. Douglass explains that the songs were difficult to understand—"apparently incoherent" to outsiders—but that the slaves themselves understood the literal meaning of the words they were singing. However, the "deep" meaning of the songs is not apparent to Douglass until he becomes an outsider to the group. Douglass implies that the "deep" meaning becomes clear only with distance and after applying tools of analysis. This distance explains Douglass's particular position of authority in the *Narrative.* Douglass not only experiences life under slavery, but he now also has the tools and the distance with which to interpret the practices of slavery for outside audiences.

The quotation further provides an example of the tension inherent in the *Narrative.* Douglass must abandon his former slave self in order to become a narrator capable of interpreting the experiences of that former self. Implicit in this quotation is the idea that a culture remains invisible to those who are raised within it. To each of us, our everyday practices seem normal—they seem to have little meaning and therefore cannot be interpreted. As such, Douglass does not understand the symbolic meaning of the slave songs when he is one of the singers. Douglass suggests that only after moving away from his culture can he gain interpretive distance from it.

3. Whilst I was saddened by the thought of losing the aid of my kind mistress, I was gladdened by the invaluable instruction which, by the merest accident, I had gained from my master.

This passage occurs in Chapter VI, after Hugh Auld orders Sophia Auld to stop Douglass's reading lessons because he feels education ruins a slave for slavery. This moment represents a minor climax of the first half of the *Narrative*. Douglass, upon overhearing Hugh Auld's words, finally realizes that whites hold blacks in their power through a series of strategies—most notably that of depriving blacks of education and literacy. To Douglass, this admission is valuable for two reasons. First, it confirms his fledgling sense that slavery is not a natural or justified form of society, but is rather a constructed power strategy supported by deprivation and dehumanization. In other words, Douglass knows himself not to be naturally inferior, but rather a victim of enforced ignorance. Second, Hugh Auld's words allow Douglass to realize, through inversion, that he must become educated to become free. This lesson about the value of education is more important than the reading lessons themselves.

This quotation also shows that Douglass associates males and females with different kinds of knowledge. Though Douglass himself was a strong women's rights advocate in later life, the *Narrative* depicts Douglass's path to freedom as a confrontation with and an adoption of male authority. Though Douglass's self-education and struggle for freedom question the dominant assumptions about power and race, they implicitly adopt the dominant assumptions about power and gender. For example, Douglass presents his climactic moment of transformation from slave to man—his fight with Covey in Chapter X—as a moment defined by male physical power. In the quotation above, Douglass's rhetorical structure sets the femaleness of Sophia Auld's reading lessons as antithetical to Hugh Auld's larger lesson *about* Sophia's lesson. Douglass presents masculine knowledge as knowledge about knowledge, superior to feminine lessons. Douglass aligns himself with Hugh Auld in this equation, both through his dedication to opposing Hugh Auld and through his dedication to obtaining a form of knowledge that he understands to be masculine.

4. My natural elasticity was crushed, my intellect languished, the disposition to read departed, the cheerful spark that lingered about my eye died; the dark night of slavery closed in upon me; and behold a man transformed into a brute!

This quotation, taken from Chapter X, shows Douglass's focus on how he was made into a slave. In one sense, the *Narrative* is the story of a slave becoming free, but it is also the story of how men are made into slaves. As the structural center of the *Narrative,* Chapter X describes Douglass's descent into the most brutal conditions of slavery and then his reaffirmation of his desire to be free. Douglass's low point as a slave occurs during the first six months of his year with Edward Covey. Covey's tactics in remaking Douglass into a slave consist mainly of incessant work and constant, brutal punishment. Douglass focuses on the mental and spiritual, rather than physical, consequences of Covey's treatment. For Douglass, it is no mystery how slave owners are able to control slaves through physical debasement. The more mysterious process, and the one that Douglass is concerned with revealing and analyzing, is the way slavery dominates the mind and spirit of a slave. Thus Douglass shows that Covey's brutality causes Douglass to lose intangible parts of himself, including his ambition to become educated. Similarly, Douglass presents his triumph over Covey later in Chapter X as both a physical and a mysteriously mental and spiritual endeavor.

This quotation also evinces Douglass's talent for rhetorical flair. The four-part repetition in the first part of the passage reinforces the way Douglass depicts his dehumanizing transformation. The final phrase of the sentence, "behold a man transformed into a brute," contains a second-person address to the reader, exhorting him or her to "behold." Douglass frequently uses this type of second-person address in the *Narrative*. It suggests that the reader must participate in the text somehow, as a witness or a judge. Finally, the imagery of the quotation evokes common light-dark imagery, in which light is positioned as representative of human reason and knowledge, while dark represents a subhuman, unenlightened state—here, the state of slavery.

5.   In coming to a fixed determination to run away, we
      did more than Patrick Henry, when he resolved upon
      liberty or death.

This passage appears in Chapter X of the *Narrative*, in which Douglass relates his plans to escape with several fellow slaves from William Freeland's. Several times in the *Narrative*, Douglass describes in detail the explicit dangers that slaves face in attempting escape. Slaves must confront natural enemies, such as the weather or dangerous animals, as well as human enemies in the form of their owners or slave hunters. Slaves are never sure of making it to free land and are not assured freedom even if they do escape and survive. Douglass focuses on the incredible dangers of escape to suggest that Northerners cannot simply rely on slaves fleeing injustice by themselves. Instead, Northerners must take political action against the institution of slavery to ensure that further escapees are not harmed.

In this quotation, Douglass alludes to patriot Patrick Henry's declaration "Give me liberty or give me death," which was made during the American fight for independence. Douglass suggests that his own bravery and that of his fellow slaves is more impressive than Henry's. Whereas Henry chose between a desirable option and an undesirable option, escaping slaves must try to guess at the lesser of two evils. Douglass also implies that slavery often can be worse than death. Slaves suffer inordinately through either their escape or their continued existence as slaves.

Douglass uses the reference to Henry to compare the slaves' quest for freedom and rights to the American Revolutionaries' crusade for rights. On the one hand, this cultural context would make the abolitionist cause seem more recognizable and familiar as a fight for fundamental rights. On the other hand, Douglass's use of Revolutionary references in the *Narrative* also ironically points to the hypocrisy of Americans. Americans take great pride in their historical establishment of a system of rights, yet they still deprive a large section of the population—slaves—of those very same rights.

Key Facts

FULL TITLE
Narrative of the Life of Frederick Douglass, An American Slave,
Written by Himself

AUTHOR
Frederick Douglass

TYPE OF WORK
Autobiography

GENRE
Slave narrative; *bildungsroman*

LANGUAGE
English

TIME AND PLACE WRITTEN
1845; Massachusetts

DATE OF FIRST PUBLICATION
1845

PUBLISHER
American Anti-Slavery Society

NARRATOR
Frederick Douglass

POINT OF VIEW
Douglass writes in the first person

TONE
Douglass's tone is generally straightforward and engaged, as
befits a philosophical treatise or a political position paper. He
also occasionally uses an ironic tone, or the tone of someone
emotionally overcome.

TENSE
Past

SETTING (TIME)
1818–1841

SETTING (PLACE)

Eastern Shore of Maryland; Baltimore; New York City; New Bedford, Massachusetts

PROTAGONIST

Frederick Douglass

MAJOR CONFLICT

Douglass struggles to free himself, mentally and physically, from slavery.

RISING ACTION

At the age of ten or eleven, Douglass is sent to live in Baltimore with Hugh and Sophia Auld. Douglass overhears a conversation between them and comes to understand that whites maintain power over black slaves by keeping them uneducated. Douglass resolves to educate himself and escape from slavery. However, he is later taken from the Aulds and placed with Edward Covey, a slave "breaker," for a year. Under Covey's brutal treatment, Douglass loses his desire to learn and escape.

CLIMAX

Douglass decides to fight back against Covey's brutal beatings. The shocked Covey does not whip Douglass ever again.

FALLING ACTION

Douglass is hired to William Freeland, a relatively kinder master. Douglass starts educating his fellow slaves and planning his escape. Douglass's plan to escape is discovered. He is put in jail and then sent back to Baltimore with the Aulds to learn a trade. Douglass becomes a caulker and is eventually allowed to hire out his own time. Douglass saves money and escapes to New York City, where he marries Anna Murray, a free black woman from Baltimore. They move to New Bedford, Massachusetts, where Douglass is eventually hired as a lecturer for the American Anti-Slavery Society.

THEMES

Ignorance as a tool of slavery; knowledge as the path to freedom; slavery's damaging effect on slaveholders; slaveholding as a perversion of Christianity

MOTIFS

The victimization of female slaves; the treatment of slaves as property; freedom in the city

SYMBOLS

White-sailed ships; Sandy's root; *The Columbian Orator*

FORESHADOWING

Douglass's concentration on the direction of steamboats traveling to Philadelphia in Chapter VIII; Douglass's premonition that his escape plans had been revealed in Chapter X

STUDY QUESTIONS & ESSAY TOPICS

STUDY QUESTIONS

1. *Is Douglass's* Narrative *an autobiography?*

An autobiography is a biography of a person written by that person, and it conventionally depicts a process of personal development. Douglass's *Narrative* is strictly an autobiography at certain points, but it exhibits conventions of other narrative genres as well. For example, at times Douglass intends his life story to stand as the life story of all slaves, or of a typical slave. When in his first paragraph Douglass tells us that he does not know his birth year, he implies that this personal information is important on a public level, an indication of how all slaves are treated by their masters. Douglass understands, though, that he cannot simply argue that the events of his life represent the experience of all slaves. Therefore, Douglass includes many stories from the lives of other slaves whom he knew and stories that he heard secondhand. Accordingly, the *Narrative* often skips around, rather than progressing in detailed chronological order. In these sections, Douglass's *Narrative* resembles not so much an autobiography as a memoir, a genre that focuses on the people or events that the autobiographer has known, or a picaresque novel, in which the various scenes reported are held together by the fact that they one character witnesses them.

 Perhaps more than anything else, Douglass's *Narrative* drops the conventions of autobiography in favor of the conventions of political or philosophical treatise. Douglass frequently cites a situation and then analyzes it at length to support a point about the treatment of slaves or about the institution of slavery. Douglass's apparent use of rhetorical styles reinforces the treatise-like quality of the *Narrative,* as some sections strongly resemble persuasive oratory. The *Narrative* does fit the conventions of autobiography at certain points, most notably during the stories of Douglass's self-education and escape to freedom. Yet it seems that the *Narrative* is intended not so much to chronicle Douglass's own coming-of-age as to persuade readers that slavery is politically and philosophically wrong.

2.   *What function do Garrison's preface and Phillips's letter serve?*

Garrison and Phillips both provide corroborating testimony that Douglass is indeed a fugitive slave and the author of the *Narrative*. Phillips, in particular, stresses the importance of this authenticity when he implies that the powerful sometimes misrepresent the powerless. Phillips alludes to the fact that most of the information Northerners have about slavery comes from slave owners rather than the slaves themselves. This selective, biased information can present a misleading picture of slavery as a benevolent institution rather than a horrendous practice. Phillips suggests that the authenticity of Douglass's *Narrative* is important because Douglass can present a rare picture of slavery as it actually is.

Garrison's and Phillips's documents also try to prepare white readers for the text, or to make the text seem comfortable and familiar to readers. Phillips's friendly letter to Douglass presents Douglass as a known entity to readers, introducing him as a character and narrator. Phillips uses his own reputation and name to put Douglass on a more intimate level with readers. Garrison and Phillips also prepare readers for Douglass's text by presenting Douglass's story in the context of the American Revolutionaries. Garrison compares Douglass's quest for freedom from slavery to Patrick Henry's demand for liberty from British tyranny. Phillips, too, compares Douglass to a courageous revolutionary because Douglass takes brave chances by publishing the details of his past at a time when he can still be recaptured. By implying that Douglass's struggle for freedom is similar to the Revolutionaries' fight, Garrison and Phillips make Douglass's text seem more familiar to readers.

Finally, Garrison and Phillips both connect Douglass's story to their own political fight for abolition. Garrison recognizes that Douglass exhibits extraordinary talent that separates him from many of his fellow slaves. However, Garrision also treats Douglass as though he is representative of all slaves. Garrison and Phillips both present Douglass as a successful example of a freed slave, Garrison suggesting that all slaves should be similarly freed. Both writers use their documents as persuasive arguments against slavery. They intend that readers should commit to the cause of freeing slaves. In taking this focus, Garrison and Phillips situate Douglass's *Narrative* not as a private account of individual growth, but as a public record of the injustice of slavery.

3.   *How does Douglass show that slavery corrupts slave owners?*

Douglass shows that slave owners constantly deny the humanity of their slaves in order to justify their ownership of human beings. To convince themselves that their slaves are not quite human, slave owners treat them inhumanely. In treating his slaves like beasts, however, the master becomes a beast himself. He often becomes piously religious so as not to see himself as a brutal, depraved wretch. But he must pervert the Bible to justify owning slaves.

Douglass depicts the negative effects of slaveholding on slave-holders through the characters of Thomas Auld and Edward Covey. Douglass shows that both these men must pretend that they are one thing while they are really another. Thomas Auld attempts to act the part of the privileged, powerful slave owner. Both the slaves and Auld himself recognize that he is only acting, and he becomes even more tortured and cruel because of his unconvincing performance. Edward Covey pretends to himself, and to God, that he is a Christian man—righteous and pious. Douglass presents both of these men as somewhat silly and pitiable in their falseness, pointing to the psychological difficulty of performing unnaturally. Slavery, because it is unnatural, has forced this difficulty upon the men who own slaves.

Sophia Auld is another example Douglass presents to depict the damaging effects of slavery on the slaveholder, as we witness Sophia's transformation from virtuous woman to corrupt slave-owner. Douglass is the first slave Sophia ever owns. Before slavery corrupts her good character, she is a kind, affectionate woman. She initially treats Douglass like a human being, discouraging his servility and educating him. But when her husband informs her that education would ruin Douglass as a slave, she begins to treat Douglass like property. Slaveholding, then, turns Sophia's kind, generous character harsh and cruel.

SUGGESTED ESSAY TOPICS

1.   What role do women play in Douglass's *Narrative*? Pay close attention to when or if female characters speak, to how female characters relate to Douglass, and to the depiction of women in relation to virtue.

2.   Analyze Douglass's treatment of Christianity in the *Narrative*. Why does he include his "Appendix"?

3.   How does Douglass describe New Bedford, Massachusetts? How does this description undermine economic arguments in favor of slavery?

4.   Think about Douglass's private speech to the ships in Chapter X. Why does Douglass recreate this speech in his *Narrative*? What do the ships represent? Why is this moment important within the *Narrative*?

5.   Analyze the various references to American Revolutionaries in Douglass's *Narrative*. How does Douglass's use of these references differ from Garrison's and Phillips's? Why is the phrase "An American Slave" included in Douglass's title?

Review & Resources

Quiz

1. Why does Douglass have no knowledge of his birth date?

   A. A fire destroyed the records
   B. His mother died when he was young
   C. Slave owners keep their slaves ignorant of their birth dates
   D. He left his personal records behind when he escaped

2. What is Douglass's probable father's name?

   A. Colonel Lloyd
   B. Ned
   C. Captain Anthony
   D. Thomas Auld

3. Why do children of a slave-owning father and slave mother have the worst lot of the slaves?

   A. They must face the cruel wrath of the slave-owner's wife
   B. They are assigned field work
   C. They are never freed
   D. They are taken from their mothers

4. What event does Douglass connect with his introduction to the horrors of slavery?

   A. His birth
   B. Captain Anthony's whipping of AUnt Hester
   C. Gore's killing of Demby
   D. Learning to read

5.   What do Colonel Lloyd's slaves call the plantation on which Douglass grows up?

   A.   Wye Town
   B.   Great House Farm
   C.   New Design
   D.   Talbot

6.   Which of the following is *not* what Douglass interprets slave songs to be?

   A.   Prayers to God
   B.   Calls to action
   C.   Testimonies against slavery
   D.   Expressions of anguish

7.   Which of the following is *not* one of the overseers under whom Douglass grows up?

   A.   Mr. Severe
   B.   Mr. Hopkins
   C.   Mr. Gore
   D.   Mr. Auld

8.   What is Douglass's main point about Gore shooting Demby?

   A.   Gore acts irrationally
   B.   Gore isoverly cruel
   C.   Whites are not punished for killing blacks
   D.   Gore thinks Demby is trying to escape

9.   Which of the following is *not* a reason Douglass is happy about the prospect of moving to Baltimore?

   A.   The Aulds are described as a kind couple
   B.   His cousin has described Baltimore as beautiful
   C.   He has no attachments at home
   D.   He is given a pair of trousers for the move

10. What is the reason for Sophia Auld's transformation?

    A.   She becomes lazy when Douglass is around to do her work for her

    B.   She becomes cruel with the irresponsible power of owning another person

    C.   She begins drinking

    D.   She senses that Douglass is becoming smarter than her son, Thomas

11. Why is Douglass grateful that Hugh Auld orders Douglass's reading lessons stopped?

    A.   Douglass does not like his reading lessons

    B.   Auld unwittingly gives Douglass the key to escape slavery

    C.   Auld betrays his fear that Douglass might escape

    D.   Douglass already knows how to read

12. Why does Douglass believe that city slaveholders are usually less cruel than rural slaveholders?

    A.   They have no fields in which to work their slaves

    B.   They are conscious of the disapproval of their non-slaveholding neighbors

    C.   They always feed their slaves enough

    D.   They are more aware that their slaves can escape

13. Which of the following is *not* one of Douglass's sources for learning how to read and write?

    A.   Neighborhood boys

    B.   Thomas Auld's copybook

    C.   Webster's *Spelling Book*

    D.   Two Irish dockworkers

14. What does Douglass gain from *The Columbian Orator*?

    A.   A plan for escape

    B.   The meaning of "chattel"

    C.   An understanding of the political argument against slavery

    D.   A sense of community

REVIEW & RESOURCES

15. From what source does Douglass learn the meaning of "abolition"?

    A.   A newspaper
    B.   A dictionary
    C.   Sophia Auld
    D.   Two Irish dockworkers

16. Why does Douglass move from Baltimore to Thomas Auld's?

    A.   Because Douglass tries to escape
    B.   Because Auld wants to punish his brother, Hugh
    C.   Because Douglass's time of service is up
    D.   Because Douglass's original owner has died

17. What is Thomas Auld's main offense as a slaveholder?

    A.   Killing slaves
    B.   Fathering slave children
    C.   Not giving his slaves enough to eat
    D.   Overworking his slaves

18. Why do the slaves call Covey "the snake"?

    A.   Because he is evil
    B.   Because he surprises them by sneaking through the
          tall grass
    C.   Because he is thin
    D.   Because his whip resembles a snake

19. In what regard is Douglass's August confrontation with
    Covey a turning point?

    A.   Douglass realizes he could escape
    B.   Douglass fights back against Covey
    C.   Douglass convinces Covey of the wrongs of slavery
    D.   Douglass proves Covey a coward

20. What service does Douglass offer his fellow slaves at
    William Freeland's?

    A.   Religious education
    B.   A means of escape
    C.   Literacy lessons
    D.   Writing letters for them

21. What happens to Douglass and the others when their escape plan is betrayed?

    A.   They are sold
    B.   They are split up
    C.   They are jailed
    D.   They are sent to Baltimore

22. Why do Douglass's fellow apprentices at the Baltimore shipyard attack him?

    A.   They thought he stole from them
    B.   They were fearful of black workers taking their jobs
    C.   They suspected him of being an escaped slave
    D.   For no apparent reason

23. How does Douglass get enough money to escape?

    A.   He hires out his time and saved money slowly
    B.   Hugh Auld gives him money
    C.   He steals
    D.   He borrows from his fiancée

24. Who helps Douglass in New York City?

    A.   No one
    B.   Ruggles
    C.   Nathan Johnson
    D.   Frederick Johnson

25. Why is Douglass surprised by New Bedford?

    A.   He has been led to believe that the North is poverty-stricken
    B.   He did not know it was a shipping town
    C.   He was not expecting to meet so many blacks
    D.   He was not expecting to get work

REVIEW & RESOURCES

ANSWER KEY:

1: C; 2: C; 3: A; 4: B; 5: B; 6: B; 7: D; 8: C; 9: A; 10: B;
11: B; 12: B; 13: D; 14: C; 15: A; 16: B; 17: C; 18: B; 19: B;
20: C; 21: C; 22: B; 23: A; 24: B; 25: A

SUGGESTIONS FOR FURTHER READING

ANDREWS, WILLIAM L., ed. *Critical Essays on Frederick Douglass.* Boston: Hall, 1991.

———. *Oxford Frederick Douglass Reader.* New York: Oxford University Press, 1996.

DOUGLASS, FREDERICK. *Autobiographies.* Ed. Henry Louis Gates, Jr. New York: Library of America, 1994

GATES, HENRY LOUIS, JR. *Figures in Black.* New York: Oxford University Press, 1987.

MCFEELY, WILLIAM S. *Frederick Douglass.* New York: Norton, 1991.

MILLER, DOUGLASS, ed. *Frederick Douglass and the Fight for Freedom.* New York: Facts on File, 1993.

SEKORA, JOHN, AND DARWIN T. TURNER, eds. *The Art of Slave Narrative.* Macomb: Western Illinois University Press, 1982.

SUNDQUIST, ERIC, ed. *Frederick Douglass: New Literary and Historical Essays.* New York: Cambridge University Press, 1990.

REVIEW & RESOURCES

SPARKNOTES
TEST PREPARATION
GUIDES

The SparkNotes team figured it was time to cut standardized tests down to size. We've studied the tests for you, so that SparkNotes test prep guides are:

Smarter:
Packed with critical-thinking skills and test-
taking strategies that will improve your score.

Better:
Fully up to date, covering all new features of the tests,
with study tips on every type of question.

Faster:
Our books cover exactly what you need to
know for the test. No more, no less.

SparkNotes Study Guides: